You.com

WITHDRAWN
BY
WILLIAMSBURG REGIONAL LIBRARY

You.com
Manage your online self for profit, image and business success

CRESTA NORRIS

WILLIAMSBURG REGIONAL LIBRARY
7770 CROAKER ROAD
WILLIAMSBURG, VIRGINIA 23188

AUG – – 2011

KoganPage

LONDON   PHILADELPHIA   NEW DELHI

Publisher's note

Every possible effort has been made to ensure that the information contained in this book is accurate at the time of going to press, and the publishers and authors cannot accept responsibility for any errors or omissions, however caused. No responsibility for loss or damage occasioned to any person acting, or refraining from action, as a result of the material in this publication can be accepted by the editor, the publisher or any of the authors.

First published in Great Britain and the United States in 2011 by Kogan Page Limited

Apart from any fair dealing for the purposes of research or private study, or criticism or review, as permitted under the Copyright, Designs and Patents Act 1988, this publication may only be reproduced, stored or transmitted, in any form or by any means, with the prior permission in writing of the publishers, or in the case of reprographic reproduction in accordance with the terms and licences issued by the CLA. Enquiries concerning reproduction outside these terms should be sent to the publishers at the undermentioned addresses:

120 Pentonville Road	1518 Walnut Street, Suite 1100	4737/23 Ansari Road
London N1 9JN	Philadelphia PA 19102	Daryaganj
United Kingdom	USA	New Delhi 110002
www.koganpage.com		India

© Cresta Norris, 2011

The right of Cresta Norris to be identified as the author of this work has been asserted by her in accordance with the Copyright, Designs and Patents Act 1988.

ISBN 978 0 7494 6198 0
E-ISBN 978 0 7494 6283 3

British Library Cataloguing-in-Publication Data

A CIP record for this book is available from the British Library.

Library of Congress Cataloging-in-Publication Data

Norris, Cresta.
  You.com : manage your online self for profit image and business success / Cresta Norris.
    p. cm.
  ISBN 978-0-7494-6198-0 – ISBN 978-0-7494-6283-3 1. Internet marketing. 2. Online social networks. I. Title.
  HF5415.1265.N67 2011
  650.10285'4678–dc22

                                      2010050259

Typeset by Saxon Graphics Ltd, Derby
Production managed by Jellyfish
Printed and bound in the UK by CPI Antony Rowe

Contents

Acknowledgements

I owe special thanks to Kitty O'Leary whose incisive interview and art expertise provided the case study for Chapter 2, Jenni Mills who understands everything, and of course Jennifer Christie and Jane Graham Maw of GrahamMaw Christie, without whom the book would never have happened.

Particular thanks to all those who contributed their time and knowledge for the case studies and ideas:

- Clare Burnett

- Gill Carrick

- Lucinda Craig

- Trish Kinane

- Dulce Merritt

- Mark Phillips

- Jas Pilgrem

- Richard Sambrook

- Nancy William.

Introduction

This will be the century of *you*.

Never has the individual had more weight in the world. Through the internet, people who have been previously silent have found voices. People who have been isolated have found friends. Political movements have mobilized online, governments have been shaken (if not actually toppled) and, whether for business or for social reasons, there has never been a more powerful time to make your voice heard around the globe. If you are not online, you are not connected.

The conversation is both intensely local and global. School students travelling the world reassure their mothers they are safe via their Facebook pages. In Iran, protesters against the regime organize street rallies using Twitter and show the world what happens when the authorities crack down. In Afghanistan, an aid worker killed while passing through a supposedly safe area had communicated her fears in her blog.

Two key ideas underpin this new form of conversation. The first is a fundamental change in the concept of 'public space'. Previously, the notion of public space implied shared, physical landscapes outside the home. Now it embraces the digital world, and indeed has far more power and resonance in that sphere than it ever could within a physical setting. A man takes off his clothes in the street. A small crowd gathers. The incident might attract a few lines in the local paper. But a man who takes off his clothes on the internet may gather hundreds of thousands of followers on Facebook.

The second idea is one that has been around in Western philosophy for some time but only now has a truly global currency. It is the sense that the individual point of view matters. The connected nature of the internet has made it possible to share conversations with people all over the world, and the accessibility of social media tools makes it easy for others to join in and respond. At a macro level, this can rally opinion and mobilize political action – a tool put to good use by the Obama presidential campaign in 2008. But just as powerful is its use by consumers, to express an opinion on products and persuade others to buy a particular brand – or not. Amazon encourages readers to review books they buy from the site. Almost any online selling operation has links to product reviews posted by individual consumers, who do not mince their words if they do not like a particular product. There used to be an old adage in business that one dissatisfied customer could lose you, on average, eight other potential purchasers via word of mouth. Today, the same principle can be numbered in thousands. There is no refuge for the business that messes up.

It can be argued that the majority of online conversations are trivial in the extreme and often time-wasting. Indeed it is hard to disagree with that view should you happen across one of the online entertainment chat threads, which can cover anything from 'Should Kylie cut her hair?' to 'What do you think of Madonna's latest adoption plans?' But to sneer at online conversation because in some instances the level of discourse is less than brilliant is to miss the point entirely. Human nature hasn't changed. People love gossip, and of course online chat will attract as wide a cross-section of humanity as have access to digital technology – which these days is very wide indeed. But the essential idea to grasp is that online conversations, at whatever level, are going on all the time. No one is isolated from it. You don't need to be famous/rich/clever/influential/intellectual to discuss and be discussed. The minute you have an online identity of any sort, you too are out there in public space. This is not always to your advantage and your online reputation is crucial to your public life.

For example, a business colleague of mine, Nick, was at the Ivy (London's most fashionable restaurant) and his usual table was no longer available. When the maitre d' was distracted by another customer Nick took a sneak look at the bookings' database and saw the word 'unemployed' against his name. Yes, it was true he had just lost his job, the information was online, and he did not get the table he had booked.

Robin is a respected oil trader. One of his team made a serious trading error, losing £10 million. As the company director Robin's name is now linked in any search about rogue traders and massive losses. Winning new business could become tricky when your name is associated with a serious trading error.

Not long ago a friend of mine, a novelist though not a particularly high-profile one, moved to a new home in a small village in the depths of the English countryside. Naturally, as one might expect when a stranger enters a close-knit community, the neighbours were interested in her arrival, and she had prepared her 'story' to satisfy their curiosity – she had left the city to find peace and quiet to write. It wasn't that she had anything to hide, but being a modest sort, she had decided to pass on a simplified version of her previous life, reasoning that to go into immense detail about the ins and outs of her past career would seem at best tedious, or at worst boastful.

Before long she was invited to tea by an elderly couple in their 90s, former farmers who had lived in the village all their lives. Over cucumber sandwiches and scones, her hostess leaned forward and said: 'So I gather you used to work for the BBC.' This was absolutely true, but not part of the story my friend had been telling the neighbours. 'How did you know that?' she asked. 'We Googled you, dear.'

The point is: if it is online, people can and will find it. The implications of this are profound. Your personal digital reputation is important. What you communicate about yourself via the internet is in the public domain, and so it is worth thinking carefully about how you present your personal profile there. That is the subject matter of this book, and over the course of its pages you will discover how to manage the information about yourself that you share with the world via the internet, as well as how to use the internet to connect with other people who share your interests. You will discover how to:

- Prepare your biography and write a vision and value statement that you can use in all your online activities.

- Create photographs and a video that present you in a flattering light.

- Understand the rules of networking online.

- Use the web to explore your creative abilities.

- Receive the information you need for work or play in the timeliest manner.

- Manage your identity online.

- Protect your online privacy.

- Become famous – within the goals that you have set for yourself.

- Create a blog or twitter and engage with your friends and followers.

- Understand how to look for jobs.

- Build your business reputation.

- Move your name higher in the search engines.

- Set up a campaign and create a petition.

- Connect and help people with similar interests to you all over the world.

The two levels of the information

This is a book that works on two levels. First, it is about the technology and techniques of controlling information online. Googling yourself is not an act of vanity (besides, everybody does it, no need to be ashamed) but an essential strategy in discovering what is out there about you. Monitoring what's being said where and by whom is the starting point for taking control of your online profile. By itself, though, monitoring is not enough. You need to understand how to use Google and other search engines so that when someone searches for information about you online, they will be directed towards positive sites rather than those that might cause you embarrassment. You also need to understand how to use social networking sites, news feeds and other online tools so that you are proactive in what is being said about 'Brand You'.

But on a more profound level, the book is also about understanding the nature of Brand You. Before you can promote yourself online, let alone take control of what is being said about you, you need to understand who you really are. You will have to look deep into your own personality and background, and make decisions about what you wish to reveal about yourself. At the very least, this could save you from posting something online you will later come to regret. More fundamentally it will help you present yourself online in a way that attracts the people you want to understand your values, interests or concerns.

This is not about inventing a 'new you' or constructing a personal profile that is 'perfect' or in any way unreal. Those who try online to be something they are not will soon be found out. Authenticity is a key element of your online persona, and just as we can tell immediately when a TV personality is insincere, or a politician is trying to dodge the issue, online there is no hiding place. Rather like children and dogs who usually seem to have an instinct for spotting the less-than-genuine, the online community is quick to discover that someone is faking it.

You could, if you were rich and famous, employ a public relations agency to sort it all out for you. But this book is about something that is subtly different from what PR firms do. It is about *taking control for and of yourself*. It is about understanding both the nature of the online world and the nature of your own soul, and no PR guru on earth can do that for you.

Welcome to you.com.

Chapter One
Getting started

Putting 'Brand You' online is so quick and easy that it will take you no longer than an afternoon or an evening. Later in this chapter you'll find out exactly how to do that, step by step, at a basic level – what I call instant action/on the spot action.

Further chapters will reveal how you can add bells and whistles to the basics and refine you.com. There will be examples of how other people use an online presence to enhance their business or their social life, to find a new job or connect with a set of like-minded people, as well as other ways to manage your online profile using more sophisticated tools. But all that comes later. For now, it's important to get going and establish yourself on at least one social networking site.

Before you jump straight in and upload your profile, there is a part of the process that shouldn't be rushed. You need to devote time and thought to determine exactly what that profile will be – the online face you will present to the world. In other words, you must arm yourself with some content, in words and pictures – the essence of Brand You.

This is certainly not something to dash through, because it is the most crucial part of the whole exercise. On it depends everything that follows. This content forms the foundation of you.com, and it is worth taking time over it now, because it will serve you over and over again, on different sites and in different contexts.

The content you need at this stage consists of three elements:

1 some good *pictures of yourself*;

2 your CV *or biography*; and

3 your own *personal vision and values statement*, which sums up the reason or reasons why you are giving yourself a presence online.

The pictures

These should be the easy part, though you should take time to find really good ones of yourself which are *up to date*. The picture you choose as your main one should be bright and well lit, attractive but not overly sexy (which can be off-putting in many contexts) and certainly not unrealistic. Tempting though it may be to post the flattering studio portrait that was taken 15 years ago, consider how you will feel (and how dishonest you will seem) when any online correspondent meets you, wrinkles and all, in the flesh. By all means choose a picture that enhances your best features and makes you look good, but also remember your friends could be posting pictures of you elsewhere that show you at your less-than-best, so airbrushing away all physical blemishes and imperfections may prove counter-productive!

If you haven't already got a head-and-shoulders shot you are happy with, it could be worth paying to have one taken by a professional. Some include make-up and hair sessions in the price for female clients, and a professional's experience in good lighting and knowing what poses look most natural will probably achieve a better result than any of your friends could, unless they are gifted amateur photographers.

Style, dress and appearance matter, and can have an impact on the impression you wish to create. While someone setting up an interest group of like-minded extreme sports enthusiasts might want to pick a shot that shows him or her windswept and active in lycra, if the same person were looking for a job online it would be advisable to use a different photo revealing a more groomed and conventional appearance. Obvious advice, maybe – but ignored by a surprising number of (unsuccessful) job applicants.

For a head-and-shoulders shot, wear something of reasonably neutral appearance that is not fussy around the neck line. Take a tip from the kind of clothes actors wear when they pose for casting-directory photos: black polo necks or a simple white shirt are popular with male actors, while women often favour plain scoop-necked tops. This is not the time for a fashion statement, because apart from anything else (like the question of whether leopard print ruffles really suit you) fashion can date a photo.

When posing for a picture, consider carefully what expression to adopt: 99 times out of 100 a relaxed smile will produce the best results – people respond best to pictures of people smiling. But it is not absolutely essential to stitch a big grin on your face. There is a convention that many writers, for instance, are photographed looking thoughtful rather than jolly, gazing into the distance. My friend the writer chose a picture that makes her look particularly intense because she writes intense, dark novels, but the same picture would be positively off-putting if she was out to find a job or a new boyfriend online.

The CV

The written content you need to upload may prove more difficult. Why do we find it so hard to talk or write simply and honestly about ourselves? Probably the truth is that few of us are entirely satisfied with ourselves. When we look in the mirror at our faces, or delve (usually in the small hours of the night) into our souls, what we tend to see are the flaws rather than the positive side of ourselves. Our dreams, put into words, sound to us silly and over-reaching. Out of sheer insecurity most people put off a proper, objective analysis of personal strengths and weaknesses, true aims and desires.

It is a fortunate man or woman who can say that they not only know themselves but can bear to explain themselves to other people without intense embarrassment. All too often, the results of self-analysis committed to words seem to come out either too modest, with the light of genuine talent hidden under a whole row of bushels, or conversely arrogant, self-obsessed and boastful.

So, how to start? The important thing is not to rush this process, so that you get it exactly right, and arrive at an online profile that is accurate, attractive to other people, and won't make you squirm some time in the future.

In some respects the CV or biography is the easy part, because it consists simply of factual content. You may already have a CV prepared, especially if you have been jobhunting, but take time to look it over again and decide not only whether it is up to date but also whether it needs any tweaking before you post it online.

Someone establishing an online presence purely to look for a job will want to upload a detailed CV, and there are many excellent books and online guides to help you achieve this. But if your purpose in going online is primarily social rather than career-driven, you will want to summarize and shorten. Aim to condense the salient points of your life in a few paragraphs. Pick out what makes you interesting and special, what will surprise, intrigue and entertain anyone who comes across your profile, as well as best serving the main purpose of why you want to be online. This kind of online biog will be more personal in the sense that it could include things you would leave out of a jobhunter's CV, like your family background. Don't bother making stuff up for effect, though. It's too easy to be found out.

As for style, the best advice is to keep it simple. By all means make it amusing if that's part of your personality. A sense of humour can be a great way to make your point (assuming it is appropriate to apply wit to the subject matter). People warm to a biog or a blog that is funny, and deploying self-deprecating wit can sometimes make it easier to write about yourself. Don't over-strain to be funny, though. Someone who is jokey all the time can become very wearing, especially if they are not as funny as they think they are, and someone who is never serious often makes others think he or she has a character flaw they are desperate to hide. If in doubt, show the piece to someone else. It is not always easy to see the effect of what you have written, and if you can find a friend whose judgement you trust, they could save you from unwittingly creating the very opposite impression from the one you had hoped for. It is hard to be told you are not very funny when you thought you had written something side-splitting, but on balance it is slightly easier to hear it from a friend before you embarrass yourself than afterwards from a stream of total strangers commenting on your posting.

The same author friend I mentioned in the introduction was asked, just after securing her first publishing deal, to write a short biography to be posted on her publisher's website. You'd think a professional writer would have no difficulty coming up with something good, but far from it. 'They asked me for no more than three lines, by teatime,' she says. 'How do you compress a whole life into such a tiny space? Unfortunately, I'd been reading a lot of Terry Pratchett that summer, and I'd been impressed by the wry, jokey style in which he'd composed his own biog for his books. I thought, I want to come across like that. Sadly, I'm not as clever and funny as Terry Pratchett. I dashed off a little para about how I'd become a writer because I found it hard to get out of bed in the mornings and do a proper job, forgetting that it would sit there for ever and ever, and be almost the first thing that anyone Googling me found out about me. I've lost count of the times I've had to assure someone, through gritted teeth, that they don't have to timetable meetings with me for afternoons only, ha ha. I really, really regret not giving it more thought.'

Exercice

As an exercise, you might try writing your own biography at different lengths. Start with the longer version of your CV, as if your were preparing for a job interview, then pare it down to three paragraphs, then finally to a three-line summary.

Next, try the exercise the other way round. Start with the three-liner, then expand outwards. It's a sure-fire way of discovering what is really important to include in your online profile, and helps you get over the embarrassment of writing about yourself.

Your vision and values statement

Your vision and values statement is almost certainly the most challenging element of the bundle and it will need careful thought. What you put into this will depend on why you want to be online. If you are looking for a job, it will be about what you can bring to the next career role you want. If you are hoping to attract a financial backer for an entrepreneurial idea, it will sum up your vision for your project and what is driving you to make it succeed. If you are trying to create a profile for a campaign dear to your heart, it will be about why you feel so strongly about this cause. If you are simply looking for like-minded friends or a life-partner, it will be more about the kinds of activities you enjoy and what sort of a person you are.

But to work well, fundamentally *all* these different kinds of vision and values statements should be about you and what makes you tick. The statement will work together with your CV or biography to draw people to you online and persuade them that you are someone they want to make a connection with. I am not going to pretend that getting either of these written elements right is easy, and if it feels easy you are probably not doing it right, because it requires you to do one of the hardest things in the world – sum up yourself and your aspirations in a paragraph or two, objectively, honestly and realistically.

First, you need to decide what your core idea is. If you find this difficult, carry a notebook around with you for a day or two and jot down your thoughts on the subject. The best ideas often come when you least expect them – in the middle of loading the dishwasher, or just as you are dropping off to sleep, perhaps. Going for a walk often helps to start the brain cells working, but don't forget to take the notebook with you. Write the ideas down as soon as you can, because they may not come back with quite such breathtaking clarity when you try to retrieve the idea from the back of your mind later on.

Once you feel you have something – a process that may take days or even weeks – take a couple of hours to sit down with your notebook and try to assemble all those random ideas into something more coherent. You will be looking to construct a paragraph that sums up what you want to achieve, and why you want to achieve it.

Here are some samples:

I'm a teacher of speech and language, working with autistic children and adults, and I believe passionately that all children have the right to be encouraged to communicate as early as possible in their lives. So I've started an online petition which I'd like you to sign to lobby the government for more resources for this neglected sector of the community.

I'm a 27-year-old mother of two who loves climbing mountains, but I'm sick of being told I'm being irresponsible by risking my life when I have a duty to be around for my children. Are there any other mothers out there who face a similar dilemma, and can we get together to discuss it?

I've written my first book, and I'm looking for a publisher. It's a story about a group of friends who travel the world by bicycle trying to do good wherever they go, but inadvertently end up wrecking the lives of everyone they meet. I'm aiming at a relatively young readership – intelligent 20-somethings who travel widely and have enjoyed *The Beach*, perhaps – but mine is not so much a thriller as a comedy of misunderstandings that should appeal to all ages. I'm prepared to send it to anyone who's interested in reading it.

The Inuit people of Northern Alaska live beyond the Arctic Circle. Their traditional way of life is threatened by climate change and the gradual melting of the polar ice caps. As an anthropologist who has made a study of their culture over many years, I feel a responsibility to alert the rest of the world to the richness and diversity of human experience we are in danger of losing unless we take individual action right now to cut emissions.

I'm in my late 40s and have over 25 years' experience planning and supervising civil engineering projects, as well as a Master's degree in mathematics. Two weeks ago, the company I've worked for over the last 15 years was taken over, and I was made redundant by the new management. Although most of my experience is in the transport sector – rail and road – my skills are easily transferable and I'm looking for similar posts in any industry, including water and power. I'm efficient, adaptable and quick to learn new skills, and I see myself possibly travelling abroad in my new role, as my family are now grown.

The longer you take to think about your online CV and your vision and values statement, the more likely you are to get it right, and come up with something that won't lurk in the ether for the rest of your life waiting to catch you out or embarrass you. Don't dash it off – take as long as you need, days or even weeks, to get it absolutely right.

There are just four rules that should be your guiding light in assembling your 'content': be honest, be simple, be brief and, having written it down, print it out (much easier to read hard copy and see it as it really is, than words on a screen) leave it overnight, read it over again the next morning, and *think about how it comes across*. Remember, you may have to live for the rest of your days with whatever you write.

Rule 1: Be honest

Honesty is always the best policy online. Above all, you need to be truthful and consistent in your online statements.

The CV is usually the place where dishonesty strikes, but be sure your sins will find you out. Inventing something about yourself because you hope it will help you win a job or make you appear more attractive to the people you want to reach will easily be exposed, because online everything tends to link. A lie about your age leaves you looking like the youngest/ oldest member of your class by several years on the Friends Reunited school site. Claiming that you were the guiding light behind Project X at your last job will easily be contradicted when a former colleague from the same firm visits the LinkedIn business site.

The same applies to sins of omission. However tempted you are to lose a line or two from your CV – that executive directorship in the company that went belly-up, the temporary job as lighting cameraman on a porn film – consider before you do so whether it could come back to haunt you. Editing and even massaging your CV for a particular job application can be acceptable, but it is unwise to deliberately conceal information that reflects badly on you and that can easily be uncovered elsewhere online.

Rule 2: Be simple

Say whatever you need to say as simply as you can. Don't over-explain yourself – too much explanation can either seem patronizing or self-justifying. Your writing style should be simple too, because that's the way good writing works. Clear language is best. Don't use over-elaborate grammar or overblown vocabulary. Never use a long word if you are not entirely sure what it means. (Equally, never say it out loud if you are not sure how to pronounce it.)

A good rule of thumb, says my novelist friend, is to write like you talk – but even more simply, and without the 'ums' and 'errs' and 'sort ofs'. Again, it's all about being authentically yourself, and not trying to pretend you are something you are not.

Rule 3: Be brief

There's no need to go on and on repeating yourself – people usually get the point pretty quickly, and the online world is all about brevity and speed.

Rule 4: Print and read it again before posting it online

Once you've read it yourself, give it to a friend or family member to get their opinion. There's no point in being embarrassed about showing it to someone – after all, they'll be able to read it when it appears online! But this is your last chance to discover if you are being too modest, too boastful or just plain naff, or whether your jokes are in bad taste.

Rogue apostrophe's and contrary, commas

Even the sharpest-eyed stickler for grammar, spelling and punctuation can miss a misplaced comma or apostrophe, but you can be sure someone among your online readers will spot it. Although online chat has its own relaxed language, caring less about punctuation or spelling in the interests of speed, there are plenty of people who will gain a less than favourable impression if you appear to be entirely unaware of the conventions of written English in a more formal setting such as your CV or vision and values statement. So again, getting a friend to 'proofread' what you have written can be very helpful.

In summary, take your time to decide what you want to write to establish your online presence – and having thought, think again after you have written, and before you post it. But the process isn't over yet. Words are all very well, but nothing works better to promote your cause than a visual statement.

The video

Using the same vision and values paragraph as the basis, make a *video version*. At its simplest, this could be you speaking directly to camera and explaining what you are about in your own words. What TV people call a 'piece-to-camera' can be very effective because it allows people to see the real enthusiasm and passion in someone's face and body language.

To do this, you need nothing more than a mobile phone with a video function, or a pocket digital camera. The better the piece of kit, of course, the better your video, but these days even quite basic equipment produces excellent quality footage of a high enough technical standard to upload to a video-sharing website.

However, a piece of equipment is still only as good as its operator, so here are a few simple rules for shooting video borrowed from the professionals that will help you produce the best possible video:

- Persuade a friend or family member to lend a hand and operate the camera.

- Film out of doors, as it is much easier and quicker to get a good result outside in natural light than indoors in artificial light.

- Indoors, sit near a window so that the light from outside falls onto your face.

- The camera should be focused on your face.

- Don't let the camera operator zoom rapidly in and out; it's distracting.

How to relax in front of the camera

You are not expected to act like a professional TV presenter in your vision and values video. Indeed it might look too stagey and false if you tried to be like one. The most important thing is to be natural and to be yourself – easier said than done for most of us.

In this, you can borrow a trick or two from TV professionals. Top presenters will tell you that the best way to relax in front of the camera is not to think of it as a camera at all, but to think of it as a person to whom you are communicating your message. If you find that too hard, just talk to your friend who is behind the camera. Concentrate not on how you look but on what you are saying.

Don't try to learn your words off by heart. If you do, you could end up looking like someone straining to recite a poem at school. Just relax and talk as you would in a real conversation – thinking about the points you want to get across rather than the exact form of words you originally wrote.

It's important not to bob about too much or fidget, but you shouldn't stay rigidly still, either. Let your head and your hands move as they would in normal conversation.

It may take several goes to achieve a version that pleases you, but most TV professionals don't get it right first take. Always choose the version in which you feel you look the most natural and at ease.

Adding other pictures to your video

Your vision and values video doesn't only have to feature you. You could make it a short 'movie' – short being the operative word, don't get carried away – by editing in other relevant pictures, over which your words will run. Video editing software is freely available on the internet, and the only limits are set by your own creativity and imagination. Another writer I know made a beautiful 60-second film about her novel on the family life of refugees, simply by filming a set of close ups – an abandoned teacup, a house glimpsed through foliage – in the lush, overgrown garden where she had lived as a child, with piano music in the background and a short, poetic voiceover listing the elements of the story.

Preparing the material for you.com may take some time, but it is time well spent laying the foundations of your online presence. But then you can progress with all speed to the next stage in the process, which will hardly take any time at all.

The nuts and bolts of getting started

First, let me reassure you that this part really is not difficult. You can finish it in an afternoon and have time left over to go to the shops or pick up the children from school, or begin after tea and still be in time to catch your mates at the pub before last orders.

Step 1: Open a Facebook account

Facebook is probably the largest and most popular social networking site online, with over 500 million users worldwide. Although Facebook was started as a tool for Harvard University students, it is now used by everyone – old and young. It's free to use, because it is funded by advertisers. To start your account you need a user name and password. You can make up a user name, but most people use their given name so that their friends and family can find them easily and see their profile page and photographs.

It is a great place to join a group of people with similar interests to yours. If you have a specialist hobby you can start your own Facebook group and ask others to join you. It is also used by companies to find new clients who will be interested in their products.

On your Facebook account, upload your biography and your vision and values statement.

Step 2: Set up a blog

A blog is rather like a website or part of a website, but is written by one person (you) and then added to by regular commentary – usually describing events or activities. So on a blog the most recent entry is the one you will see first. Some blogs are commentaries on news while others are more like an online diary.

You can choose interactive blogs, where visitors who read the blog can leave messages and comments. Most blogs link to other material online. There are art blogs, music blogs and audio blogs – more about those later in the book – but as this is the 'quick start', when you set up your initial blog you could simply upload your vision and values statement.

To find a blog space you can Google Free Blog and see the list that pops up, or ask friends which blog sites they use. Or for a quick start try one of these:

WordPress (**http://wordpress.com**): free and doesn't use advertisements. You don't have to install anything.

Posterous (**http://posterous.com**): very simple to use as you can e-mail your content and it arrives on the site.

Blogger/BlogSpot (**http://blogger.com**): very easy to update your material and better still you can delete comments that are left on the site.

LiveJournal (**http://livejournal.com**): this is used by writers to compare their work.

Step 3: Open a LinkedIn account

LinkedIn is a business-oriented site for professional networking, with more than 45 million registered users across 170 countries. It aims to maintain the contact details of people in a business network.

Visit **www.linkedin.com** and open the LinkedIn sign-in page. Fill in the information using your biography and vision and values statement and make a link to your blog. Every time you update your blog it will update LinkedIn. Once you are a member you can add contacts and connections.

Step 4: Open a YouTube account

YouTube is the biggest of the video sharing sites and is owned by Google. Youtube.com is the place to start. Go into the 'sign into YouTube now' – if you don't have a Google mail (gmail) account you will need to create one and then use your Google account password to get going. To create the account, you need to give information about your location. You will get a confirmation that goes to your e-mail. Keep the gmail account for your video-sharing profile.

Next, click on the edit channel and upload your biography and your vision and values statement. Afterwards you can change the look and feel using Channel Design, or you might prefer to keep it simple and use the YouTube default systems. Upload your vision and values video and it will be displayed on the homepage. Don't forget to save your work! Follow YouTube instructions to embed your blog text within your video.

Step 5: Open a Twitter account

Twitter allows its account holders to send and read other users' messages, known as 'tweets'. Tweets are text-based posts of up to 140 characters and they are placed on the users' profile page. Many clever people love tweeting because they see it as an intellectual discipline to find something interesting to say that can be compressed into such a short space – rather like composing a haiku poem.

All your tweets will be visible to everyone in the default setting, unless you restrict them to your 'friends' list. When you have an account you can subscribe to other people's tweets and become a 'follower' of a tweeter.

Use the same CV or biography and vision and values statement, linked back to your blog, and use your real name for the username. You can use capital letters to make it more attention-grabbing. If your name is already in use, you could add your middle initial, but try not to use hyphens, spaces or numbers.

There are various ways you can use Twitter to enhance your online presence, such as sending a tweet about your video on YouTube. Having set up your account, go to the tweet aggregator. After you have downloaded the software, you can identify ideas and people that match your interests in your vision and values statement, and you might want to follow their tweets. Then add your own tweets that are based on something interesting you have thought or done.

Creating links

(See also Chapter 7.) Now you have the basics in place for your own online persona. Before you do anything else, *check the links to all the accounts.* The idea is to make everything work together, so that if you update one, all your other networking accounts update simultaneously.

The rules of networking online

The more you help other people, the more they will help you. If you have a rich and varied personal life, you will have the same online.

Be *open and honest* with people you meet in real life and in your online life. Online is a two-way relationship, but other people can see your communications so you must always be circumspect about what you say. You should always *be responsive*, which means listening to what other people have to say, and asking them questions.

Keep abreast of new topic areas that are important to your own vision and values. Link to them from your blog, and remember to ask other contacts what they think about the ideas, then respond to their thoughts.

Finally, a few thoughts on the etiquette of meeting people online – which, although in some respects freer, is almost identical to the etiquette of meeting people in real life (ie, the physical business or social sphere). If you want to meet someone you don't know but would like to have contact with, ideally you need to find someone to connect you. What matters is who actually makes the introduction. Whether the person you want to meet is a top business executive, a famous writer or rock star, you are best connected by someone they admire and trust. If you meet someone in real life, use online networking to follow up and add them to your contacts.

Finally, online as well as in real life, be prepared to face rejection occasionally. When people don't want to be your 'friend' or link to you, don't take it personally. A 'no' might be for all sorts of perfectly good reasons you are not aware of. They may be working hard and hit the wrong response button, they may be planning to leave that networking site, or they may simply have forgotten who you are. Some people are more cautious than others in the way they use social or business networking online, just as some people are more openly friendly in real life while others prefer to be more private.

Whatever happens, don't sulk. Make sure that if you meet them again online you treat them with respect, and they will probably respond favourably. Never say something rude in reply as everyone will know that you are a bad loser. In the future there might well be people whom you don't want to have contact with, and you will not necessarily want to have to explain your reasons.

When rejecting other people, however, always treat them politely. Because you are not physically face to face, the internet often makes people think they can be as rude as they like, both about and to others. The world is a pleasanter place if people treat each other with respect but, just as important, the person you are discourteous to today might be the person who holds the key to tomorrow's opportunity.

Action for getting started

- Prepare your own material:
  - check that your biography is going to work across all your activities;
  - write your own mission statement (what your vision and values are);
  - create your own video or photographs.

- Set up accounts that link to each other:
  - Facebook;
  - YouTube;
  - Twitter;
  - LinkedIn;
  - a blog.

- Ensure that the information you upload is consistent across each of your accounts.

Chapter Two
Unlocking your creativity

You.com is about showcasing your interests – and your talents. With the basics set up, as described in the last chapter, you are already a long way towards keeping your friends informed about your activities and expanding your social networks through Facebook, Twitter and LinkedIn. But there are many more ways you can use the internet to keep up with what interests you, make contact with new people and enhance Brand You – and there are also many creative tools available that can help you personalize your online presence.

The internet offers many resources that are particularly useful to creative people. Whether you are a poet, painter or potter, a musician or video artist, there will be ways you can explore not only how to bring your work to the attention of more people but also to expand the way in which you work creatively and find new ways of expressing yourself. Even if you don't think of yourself as a particularly creative person, or if you are online purely for business reasons, there will be ways you can improve you.com by tapping into those same resources.

To see just some of the ways in which you can find creative opportunities online, take a look at how one visual artist makes use of the internet.

CASE STUDY Clare Burnett

Clare Burnett is an abstract artist. She began her career by studying architecture at Cambridge, later enrolling at art school in her 20s. She is interested in shapes and colour, rather than narrative painting, and fascinated by how placing simple, pared down shapes, in the contemporary urban environment, makes viewers look differently at their surroundings.

'It's a less is more approach with simplicity encompassing and revealing complexity,' she says. Having experimented with simple shapes on a flat canvas, she eventually started cutting them out and working in three dimensions. 'At that point I began putting the shapes within buildings, within different spaces, seeing how a series of simple shapes appeared against each other, how changes made big differences and led to different readings of the space.'

Creativity is not in one box

There are three aspects to her work. First, there is experimental work she undertakes in her studio, which is often the seedbed for bigger projects in the urban environment. At the moment, for instance, having noticed how much of our everyday environment is coloured grey, she is making a series of paintings in different shades and textures of grey. 'I've returned to a kind of career-long fascination with rectangles,' she says. 'In a sense we see the world through a frame, and that's one of the concepts I'm playing with.'

Secondly, she has an umbrella creative enterprise called The Office of Art and Ideas, which covers the work she does in and around buildings and streets in the city, to encourage people to look differently at their surroundings. This work doesn't always have Clare's name attached to it; she relishes the anonymity as it gives her a more 'neutral' space and enables her to invite other artists to collaborate with her.

Associated with both of these activities, she is sometimes invited to do residencies or exhibitions, or undertake particular projects for a client. And thirdly, she does some education work, particularly with 14- to 19-year-olds, which she says often helps inform her own projects.

Develop your own network

Being an artist of any kind often feels like a rather solitary existence, and it is easy to become isolated. But most artists relish contact with others, and find that their creative projects are enriched by being able to discuss their work with other people, or take on collaborative enterprises.

Traditionally, in order to make contacts not only with buyers but with other artists, artists like Clare were dependent on galleries, where their work would be exhibited in a formal way. Many would, and still do, take on teaching roles in art colleges, simply to have a forum in which they could discuss their ideas with other people. Clare, as well as keeping in touch with her former tutors and fellow students, has a role on the Council of the Royal Society of Sculptors, and through membership of that and similar organizations, has been able to network and find support.

Turn bricks and mortar into clicks and blogs

'Open studios' are another traditional way of keeping in touch creatively, where a group of artists throw open their studios and invite others in to see their work. Again, this is often not so much about selling work as a way of keeping in touch creatively. In order to reach an even wider range of contacts, some artists would write about their work, publishing their own books, or would keep in touch with other artists elsewhere in the world by letter. Sometimes that kind of communication became a creative exploration in itself. 'There have always been quite a lot of mail art projects,' says Clare, 'where artists might ask others to submit something on a postcard and they'll make an exhibition of it.'

Nevertheless, it could still be a lonely life as an artist, especially if you lived some distance from a creative centre. The internet has changed all that for many. Networking with other artists online can be a great support and source of ideas, and the internet is a wonderful showcase for almost all creative enterprises.

Clare has three separate websites to display what she does and also a blog, hosted by blogspot.com, to keep others abreast of progress in her current work.

Using creative design

One website is an overview of her studio work, with photos of the kind of drawings, paintings and sculptures she has created in the studio, showing the different themes that interest her. The design of the site itself, with its simple circles and rectangles against solid colour backgrounds, reflects her style as an artist and of course is fluid and likely to change as her ideas change.

Clare designed it herself: 'For a long time I had a site created by a fantastic web designer, but in the end I realized it wasn't representing exactly the way I wanted to carve the online space up. So I redid it myself, using iWeb on my Mac. It can be frustrating to do it yourself, as there may be things you want but can't do, and you have to use and adjust the templates it offers you, but I like the fact that I can just quickly do it and upload it.'

From this website there is a link to her blogspot and to the other websites she has set up. You can also click to follow her on Twitter.

The second site covers work she has done under the umbrella of her Office of Art and Ideas – sculptures in situ, mostly in the urban environment – though her name is not directly attached to it. This website is entirely separate and doesn't link back to the studio website, as Clare wants to keep her two different artistic personae separate, even though they feed on the same ideas.

The third site is called 'Art For Education' and is about the artist-led service for schools that Clare has set up. It creates artworks in school buildings and playgrounds to raise pupils' awareness of the visual arts, and also delivers art workshops and training for Key Stages 1–4 and 16+. There are pictures of the temporary and permanent installations Clare and her fellow artists have created on school premises with the help of pupils.

Posting on Facebook

Clare updates her blog whenever she feels like it, often talking not only about work in progress but also about the kind of exhibitions she has been to see, or campaigns she has become involved in. Whenever she posts something there it also automatically appears on her Facebook page.

'You can follow me on the blogspot, but more people follow it via Facebook,' she says. 'I can update the blog from my phone, so if I see something that interests me while I'm out and about, I take a photo of it and send it through to the blogspot, and write something about it there and then. It's for other people to look at, but it's also very useful for me too, as a record of what I was looking at and thinking about while I was making a particular work of art. So I can look back and see what was influencing me while I was doing something, even though I may not have realized at the time what that idea came out of.'

Clare is very definite that this use of the blog is not in any sense an online diary. 'I'm quite careful. I don't put everything online. But sometimes I like to take stock of the work I'm doing and so I write a piece about it. Of course, on the blog you do have the option of deleting stuff later, so occasionally I might go back and decide that I don't want to leave what I've written there. I think of the blog very much as about work in progress, and what I'm thinking or doing that influences my work – whereas my website is less fluid, as it only features work that is already finished and resolved.'

Although Clare's websites are part of her identity as an artist, and a way of networking with other people interested in what she is doing, they also help her market her work. The studio website is the place that people would go if they wanted to buy an existing piece of her work. But if they wanted to commission her to take on a project for them – indoors or out – they would approach her via The Office of Art and Ideas. 'I'm not selling directly via my website. If I had prices all over the site, that would look too commercial, and it would alienate other artists who come to the site to find out what I do rather than to buy. But of course artists need to make money somehow, and there is a marketing job to do for my work, though I want to spend as little time as possible on that. So in a sense the websites do the marketing for me, simply by being a space where I can direct people who want to see what it is I do.'

Sharing ideas

For Clare, though, selling her work isn't the main reason she's online. 'It's a reference space and for sharing ideas. Another artist might say, "I'll take a look at your website", and then start a conversation about our approaches to work.'

Being online has even shaped the artistic work Clare now does. She has no formal training in IT, but she isn't afraid of computers and has learnt by doing. She uses Photoshop a lot. 'Often I do a drawing and scan it in. Then I might move it around using Photoshop, or overlay it on a picture of the site if I am working on a commission. Then I print out the result and do more work on it. So I use the computer as an artistic tool in quite a fluid way, going backwards and forwards from pencil and paper to computer-aided design.'

It has also influenced her artistic choices in another way, triggering a new set of creative concepts that spring directly from being online. 'The ideas I'm playing around with at the moment – the grey rectangles – came out of the fact that so much of what we see comes to us on a screen – television screens, mobile phone screens, computer screens. I'm fascinated by the screens of computers, especially as they switch on and off. I even play with 'sketchbook' on my mobile phone to help me visualize my ideas, and I have done a lot of work that is actually about the physical forms of mobile phones themselves. I often work on shapes that have become a norm within our environment, so much so that we almost don't take any notice of them, but I like to make us aware of the forms we are filtering out.'

Although Clare has a presence on Twitter and Facebook, they are linked in to her websites, which she sees as the primary space where she showcases herself and her work. 'I decided to have a space where I could put stuff so that it wouldn't get too confusing, and where people could come to see what I am doing. What I like about this way of being online is the feeling that I am completely in control of everything.'

The nuts and bolts of being creative

So being online offers a creative person a whole range of possibilities – a way to network with other artists, a place to showcase work, and even the tools to create the art itself. How might you follow Clare's example and use the internet to unlock your creativity?

Explain your ideas visually

The great thing about online creative tools is that they work equally well for artists or business people. You don't have to be a technical wizard to use them – as a virtual artist you're not going to need to rush into town to buy lots of paint brushes. Creative programmes are ready to use with a click of your mouse. We all know that an idea that is explained visually is often stronger than one explained in words. So an easy-to-manipulate visual system is extremely useful for building your reputation online. Below is a run-through of some of the visual and creative tools available that you need to be aware of when you start your creative online communications.

Creating a website

If you want to play at creating your own website, as Clare did, Yola.com has tools to build a website based on a point, click, drag and drop process. It incorporates Google maps, text and pictures and shows the low barriers to entry of website design, so you don't need a web designer to be creative: you can do this from your home office. Clare created her own website on her computer and then uploaded it using the Transmit software program to her host server for which she pays a small monthly fee.

Using creative materials

Like many creative people, Clare sometimes uses 'found' objects or other artists' material to 'sample' and incorporate into her own work. If you have found material online that you would like to reuse in your work (assuming that there are no copyright issues – and please do check first, and ask permission before using it, as this can be a contentious area) – you will need to look at the type of browser that you are using.

The Firefox web browser works with an 'open source' coding that allows application developers to create new devices. Open source means that the software licence makes source code available to everyone, and does not have any restrictions on its use: you can copy what is on the screen and make a screen grab of the pictures or material you have found. This is useful for business purposes where you want to show your colleagues the material you have researched. Internet Explorer is also a web browser, but the coding sources are closed so it has fewer tools that allow you to manipulate the material you view.

Twitter is another open source system so allowing developers to create applications. You will read about using Twitter later on, but in creative terms the great thing about Twitter is that it has many visual applications. For example, TrendsMap uses Twitter to tell you what is being discussed worldwide at any moment in time. You can click into the feed to see exactly what is being said at any place worldwide. TwitterFall offers a changing list of all the topics being discussed – journalists use the TwitterFall to see what is news, because if something is being talked about it is usually news. The London *Telegraph* newspaper has a Fall Wall in its office alongside the TV news feeds.

What makes Twitter interesting to business as well as art is that you can see what is happening in real time, so it is one of the best forms of research about a product or idea. This makes it a useful way of finding individuals who are interested in your ideas or your product or who might become brand ambassadors and join your loyalty programme.

Similar to Twitter, several search engines allow you to search for images and understand their visual associations. As with a word search, you type in the word or object name; they then allow you to see the image and create a wall of images that intensify the word or brand you are searching for and any visual associations of the word or brand. Best known is **www.spezify.com**, and Google also has its own picture search system called Insight.

Creative sites online

If you are looking at creating movies but only have still photographs, an easy place to begin is with Animoto. It's free to use (although you have to pay for upgrades) but better still it is very simple. You upload your pictures, choose a piece of music from your collection and the Animoto system mixes them together in a short presentation.

If you need to save the videos you can do so on Keepvid.com which allows you to download any video rather than saving it on YouTube.

Many Eyes is a website based on encouraging sharing and conversation about visualizations. Many Eyes is a system that uses data to create visualization and so enable a new social kind of data analysis. The idea behind Many Eyes is that when you place lots of dull data on a screen they are hard to understand, but when you transform them with graphics they can show all sorts of unexpected patterns. Like many artists the creators of Many Eyes believe that visualization is a catalyst for discussion and collective insight. You can view other people's collections or upload your own data from a spreadsheet or a word file and visualize it.

Wordle is another visualization process that creates 'word clouds' from text that you provide. You will probably recognize the format as word clouds are popular with creative designers – and Wordle allows you to create your own. The clouds give greater prominence to words that appear more frequently in the source text. You can tweak your clouds with new colours, change of fonts and layouts. The images you create with Wordle are copyright-free under a Creative Commons Attribution licence, so you can print T-shirts, business cards, or add the image to your website.

This is just a taste of some of the online creative tools that exist to enhance you.com. You will find plenty more if you search for them, and once you are up and running online, other people might have suggestions that could help. If you see something you like, don't be afraid to e-mail someone and ask them how they did that. Most people online are happy to share ideas, and as Clare found, the best way to learn how to be in the online space is by getting out there and trying things.

The only limits to online creativity are the ones you impose on yourself!

Action for creatives

- Don't fit yourself into a box – you can do whatever you want; use different websites to show different elements of your work or ideas.

- Think in pictures not words.

- Create your own website.

- Use open source coding if you want to display pictures from other sites.

- Research creative tools – Wordle, Many Eyes, Animoto, TrendsMap.

Chapter Three
Getting informed

As well as allowing you to express your creativity, and to network with friends and new contacts, having an online presence is about keeping informed. You.com allows a two-way flow of information – information about you to the world, and information about the world to you.

The web has information for everyone. It is not just about rolling news and current affairs. In business, you may need to know what your competitors are releasing or to keep track of industry news. Professionals could use online information as an ongoing training resource to keep up with the latest developments in their field. A doctor will want to know what the medical journals are discussing this month; a lawyer will want to know the latest court rulings that might affect an ongoing case. Patients with chronic conditions might be looking to keep abreast of the latest health developments. Or on the lighter side, you might choose to have a 'fun' stream of sports and music fed to you via the internet.

Again, the key is linkage. If you are surfing many different websites to stay up to the moment with the latest industry information, now is the time to stop. Instead, your next task is to create an information stream that is relevant to you, your interests, or your business. And there's no better way to find out what you might do than turn to the example of a man whose business is information. Along the way, you'll also get some useful tips on the best way to disseminate your own information stream, via your blog, and the dos and don'ts of successful blogging.

CASE STUDY Richard Sambrook, Global Vice Chairman and Chief Content Officer, Edelman and former Director of the BBC's Global News division

There are probably only a handful of individuals who need to connect with as many people as Richard Sambrook while he was at the BBC. Working in a fast-changing international environment, Richard was responsible for all of the BBC's global news operations. He had to create a clear, coordinated presence in international media, improving the impact of BBC journalism with global audiences in a division that contains BBC World Service radio, BBC Monitoring, BBC World News television and the BBC's international online news services.

He used the digital world in three different ways:

1 to stay informed, which is no small task given the fast-changing agenda of international news;

2 to manage his identity online and present his independent voice;

3 to keep in touch with the 2,500 people worldwide who report to him.

This case study will tell you how he did it, and his tips for making it as straightforward and easy as possible. Richard's field is media and journalism, but the strategy he used could be applied in medicine, finance, law and international retail. Richard follows the news continually, but he spends *only 20 minutes, two or three days a week* on his blog and Twitter communications.

Staying informed

Richard works at a computer for most of the day, and also has an iPhone when he is out and about. He monitors the BBC news on the BBC news site, and he keeps an eye on the BBC's main competitors. His main source of information is a News Reader, a software program that collates different data feeds together in one place. His News Reader is 'Net News Wire' and he has it routed to both his laptop and iPhone. It pulls together the 200 different personally chosen feeds, blogs and sources, which he organizes rather like a traditional newspaper – main news, business, sport and fun (his personal interest in music and photography). His News Reader gives him headlines from UK newspapers where he is based, and he receives feeds from *The New York Times*, *The Washington Post*, *The*

Jerusalem Post and many other newspapers. Every day he scans the headlines and picks out a handful of stories to review. He does the same with chosen columnists – from Tom Friedman in the United States to Simon Jenkins in the UK.

Also organized into areas of interest are carefully chosen international blogs, ranging from comment on large commercial sites to individual blog writers with strong views. When Richard doesn't have time to read the article, he bookmarks it for a later date.

So how does he decide which 250 different feeds he should be looking at? Personal recommendations are the main criteria. Increasingly, he follows suggestions from Twitter. While blogs and other sites are similar to static notice boards, Twitter is real-time flow of conversation and discussion. Richard has built up a community of people whose ideas he is interested in, and they share links to material they want to discuss. Richard admits: 'Originally I was scathing about Twitter. At first you don't understand what it's about – when you subscribe and there is simply a question which says, "What are you doing?" There are a lot of people who say, "11 o'clock, time for another cup of tea", and you think what on earth is the point of that?'

However, he soon built up a list of people whose comments he watches in particular. 'I follow about 700 people on Twitter, and I have about 3,000 people who follow me. It starts with people you know, it builds out to people you know of, and then it extends to people *they know*, and then there is a *whole crowd of strangers* who for some reason think they'd like to know what you're saying.'

For Richard, this has created a rich seam of information. For example, he follows the New York University Professor Jay Rosen, a professor of journalism, and an innovative thinker in the digital world. Professor Rosen uses Twitter purely for professional reasons, and his tweets link to a blog written by one of his students, Cody Brown, a 20-year-old at New York University. Richard describes himself as: 'A 50-year-old managing a legacy media operation, trying to reinvent it for a new generation.' So Cody Brown's blog, which comes from the perspective of a 20-something who has never lived without the internet, provides him with an essential perspective – and in turn Cody has links that Richard says he would probably never have found other than through those recommendations and those connections.

Richard recommends Twitter at a professional level for linking innovative intellectual ideas and for information gathering. He says: 'People witness things – they will say, "Look at what I've just seen", and there will be a link to a picture. Remember the plane that landed in the Hudson in New York? The first picture of that came via Twitter, which was then used by all the news organizations.' He uses Twitter 'hash tags' to filter and search for particular material – this is a search function where you add the hash key (the symbol Americans use for 'number') before a tag or word you are searching for.

Managing identity online

Richard believes it's important to keep an eye on how you are represented on the web. He recommends that anyone with a senior role should set up a news feed based on their name to alert them when they are mentioned on the internet. Representing the BBC and the World Service can be controversial, and he needs to know what people are saying about him. He believes that managing an identity online is something all managers should be active about, particularly if they are in a public role.

For example, his profile on Wikipedia contained a number of errors. When he attended conferences and panel discussions the same phrases were being used in his introduction – and they were incorrect. He says: 'I kept thinking, where do people get this from? It wasn't my CV or anything else – and then I worked out it was coming from Wikipedia. Lots of people don't want to go to a lot of trouble preparing an introduction, so they just say to themselves: "Oh, Wikipedia, here it is, I'll read it out". And of course it was wrong.'

He will also intervene in blog discussions. He joins the discussion and takes responsibility for his business decisions. He admits that sometimes comments or the participants are offensive, but more often people respect the fact that he has responded and is being open and transparent. Working for a public organization, he recognizes the need to actively manage the organization's presence on the internet.

Richard also uses his own blog to correct misinformation. For example, one of his duties is to appoint the person who runs the BBC World Service. A London evening newspaper announced that the vacancy was 'stitched up' and that he was going to appoint himself! He says: 'Of course I phoned the *Evening Standard* and told them they were factually wrong: that I was appointing the person, and was not a candidate for the job – and they agreed a correction somewhere on the bottom of page 47 in tiny print.' However, using his blog he could explain what had happened. 'So people within the media industry no longer think: "What's Sambrook up to? Something fishy going on there." They think: "Oh, I understand what's happening here now."' The blog ensures that he is not dependent on newspapers choosing when and where they correct their mistakes.

Staying in touch

Richard has a blog on sambrook.typepad.com called SacredFacts based on the quote, 'Everyone is entitled to his own opinion but not to his own facts' from Daniel Patrick Moynihan. He blogs a couple of times a week. Sometimes he writes about new ideas and people or places he has visited. At other times he uses the social bookmarking site Delicious (**http://delicious**) to automatically feed to his blog links to articles and blog posts he is interested in.

He believes that his blog gives him an independent voice. The 2,500 people who work for him are not forced to read it – and he is not wasting their time with a newsletter to throw in the bin, or an e-mail to delete. The blog is aimed at those who want to know his priorities and interests about key issues in the news media industry. He says: 'People discovered that I am not a remote figure, but someone who talks about things relevant to their work in an informal way. I started with a blog which was within the BBC system, behind the BBC firewall. After three months I asked the IT team to check if anybody was looking at it. To my amazement, they said you have more than 6,000 different people a month looking at it within the BBC. Now my own division is just 2,500 strong, so I had people significantly beyond my division within the BBC interested. I'd be in the lift and people would talk to me about it. So it was clearly an effective way of communicating internally. Later I decided to make it available outside the BBC as well.'

Richard thought long and hard about communicating direct on the public internet, but has found it a very positive experience. He considers carefully what he writes, and in particular the tone of his thoughts. He says: 'Of course there are things that I would never blog about. In management at the BBC there are discussions that I'm not going to reveal – and the same would be true for any professional.'

However, he is convinced that a blog cannot be an extension of a PR department, made of corporate messages. He has a quick checklist for a Director or CEO who wants to start a blog:

✔ Feel comfortable in the balance between the personal and the professional. Do you want to talk about your family or is it better not to expose them in public? Do you want it to be primarily about your work or about your private interests?

✔ Engage your readers with your personality. It has to feel authentic and not too polished.

✔ Be transparent and open. Readers can tell when you are holding back.

Richard may be a journalist but he believes that you do not need to be a professional writer to be a great blogger. However, you must be comfortable with the line between the professional and the personal, and you need the desire to communicate and connect with people. He says: 'If you are a senior manager in a big and complicated organization, blogging or the live conversation of Twitter is one of the most effective ways of trying to connect to people. I now know a group of people in their late 20s and early 30s who are obviously far more conversant in internet and social media than I am. That is hugely enriching and their perspective is incredibly valuable to me as a senior executive. The internet is transforming business. We are at the very early stages of a profound disruption in the way we have traditionally communicated, and the beginning of a golden age for information.'

The nuts and bolts of information

So how do *you* set about creating an information stream that is relevant to your interests or your business? First, you need to understand a few technical terms, and the different kinds of information streams that exist.

RSS

Information is free, but some information streams are supported by advertising – don't be put off by this; often the advertisements are relevant to your business or interests and give you information that you need. The technical terms for the web content format that delivers information to your desktop is RSS or Really Simple Syndication.

RSS feeds are marked on a website or blog with an orange icon. When you click on them you will receive an e-mail every time a site updates its content, so you don't have to constantly surf all the sites you are interested in to stay informed. And the RSS doesn't just work for information. It can update you on Music (**www.music.com**) and take you to the latest tracks from your chosen artist, or Video Alerts (**www.video-alerts.com**) will let you know when new videos are uploaded that may be relevant to your work or company – for example you might need to view your competitors' new advertisements, or watch key executives from your industry being interviewed.

Richard uses the desktop software Net News Wire, but a feed reader is available through search engines such as the Google reader, the Yahoo reader, as well as feeds from browsers such as Mozilla Firefox and Internet Explorer, and e-mail software such as Microsoft Outlook 2007 and Mozilla Thunderbird. Feeds such as Digg and Reddit will let you search for submitted stories that match your interest on websites, while Technorati will track mentions of your interest on social networking sites like Facebook or LinkedIn.

Even blog conversations can be tracked and picked up by using Blogpulse's feed, and BackType allows you to search for comments from a named blogger and will send a message when a new comment has been posted. If you want to share information on a blog you can bookmark it, as Richard does, using the online bookmarking service del.icio.us to share bookmarks online.

BoardTracker is s message board monitoring tool that allows you to keep track of forum posts and topics, and will also include forum names (which would be useful if you are following a particular subject or need to know what is being said about a particular company). If you want to search on Twitter you can use its search engine and RSS feed using the hash key before the key word for which you are searching.

Google offers alerts in a range of different categories: if you go to its website you will see that it categorizes the material into 'News', 'Web', 'Blogs', 'Comprehensive', 'Video' and 'Groups'. This is how Google describes its service:

- A 'News' alert is an e-mail aggregate of the latest news articles that contain the search terms of your choice and appear in the top 10 results of your Google News search.

- A 'Web' alert is an e-mail aggregate of the latest web pages that contain the search terms of your choice and appear in the top 20 results of your Google Web search.

- A 'Blogs' alert is an e-mail aggregate of the latest blog posts that contain the search terms of your choice and appear in the top 10 results of your Google Blog search.

- A 'Comprehensive' alert is an aggregate of the latest results from multiple sources (News, Web and Blogs) into a single e-mail to provide maximum coverage on the topic of your choice.

- A 'Video' alert is an e-mail aggregate of the latest videos that contain the search terms of your choice and appear in the top 10 results of your Google Video search.

- A 'Groups' alert is an e-mail aggregate of new posts that contain the search terms of your choice and appear in the top 50 results of your Google Groups search.

Obviously, what determines the information you receive will be the key words you use to search for it. Put aside some time for trial and error as you try out different words, and scan the headlines of the material you are sent to see if it is relevant to your needs. If you are working in a different language it is also possible to set the alert to the language of your choice.

Conference alerts

Occasionally you might want to follow or monitor a web page that doesn't allow an RSS feed for changes that have been made. WatchThatPage.com. will send an alert if any change is made to that page. Once you are used to using the alert process you can start looking for other information that will make your business life easier – for example **www.conferencealerts.com** will e-mail updates of conferences matching your interests, available dates and preferred destinations. Conference alerts are useful if you are planning to find speaking engagements to increase your image in real life as well as online. When you speak at a conference your name will be on the agenda, and often your speech is placed online afterwards either as a written PDF document or as a video feed.

Weather alerts

On a daily basis weather alerts are useful if you have a business that is weather-dependent – if you are a builder or a wedding planner you will need to predict the weather to ensure you can work to the best of your ability. The US company **www.severealerts.com** has a Rain-Alert service that delivers updates to companies that work outside, alerting them when rain is falling within 60 minutes travel of the job site. There are also alerts for more severe weather scenarios – tornado, thunderstorm, flash flood, snow and other warnings – that go straight to your e-mail or mobile phone.

To have a complete picture of what is happening in the area that interests you, you might need to follow social media – a system called Social Mention allows you to enter a key word and switch between conversations on Twitter, bookmarks, comments and images. Alternatively you can use the Facebook Lexicon to search any key word and see how it is discussed on Facebook users' 'walls'.

You.com alert

Finally, it is worth mentioning that many people use feed readers to track their own names, just to check that online material about them is accurate and appropriate. You need to know about any mistakes so that you can correct them, as soon as possible after they are posted. If you have a public role and a Wikipedia entry then you might want to track change history for your Wikipedia page and have the changes sent to your RSS reader. As we'll see in the next chapter, a key aspect of managing your online identity is taking control of how, where and in what guise you appear on the internet.

Action for information

- Set aside 20 minutes, three days a week.

- Decide if you want to have an independent voice.

- Complete Richard's checklist – do you really want to blog?

- Decide the level of information you need on the RSS feeds.

- Set alerts to track information you need – news alerts, weather alerts, your own name alerts.

Chapter Four
Getting control

Gatekeeping your online privacy

Although it is almost impossible not to have an online presence in the 21st century, not everyone welcomes it. What one person sees as making their mark on the world, another may see as bordering on personal intrusion.

Today's culture is very different from the one previous generations grew up in. This is an era where celebrities happily share their heartbreak, their 'drug-hell' weaknesses, their sexual ambiguity and their children's illnesses. People routinely share information our grandparents' generation would have blanched at. Being 'open' is seen as a virtue. Being 'discreet' is felt by some people these days to be even a little dishonest.

So it is easy to be carried away by the confess-all culture into thinking that everything should be shared. However, although allowing an online presence to reveal your humanity may often be desirable, and can help promote your business, it is also worth remembering that discretion has its good points too. Our grandparents had a phrase for it: don't wash your dirty linen in public. By which they didn't just mean the downright grubby. They also believed there was very little value in washing even the 'once-worn' under other people's gaze.

This chapter covers what can be done to maintain your personal boundaries online: in other words, how to gatekeep you.com. It will look at why some people might want to have a lower profile online, and how that can be achieved.

To begin, here's a short personality test:

Test

1   The doorbell rings. A glance through the peephole reveals a neighbour on the doorstep, holding a parcel she has taken in on your behalf. Do you:

   A   Ignore the bell and pretend you are not in?

   B   Invite her in for a cup of coffee or glass of wine?

   C   Thank her, take the parcel, and close the door?

2   On a long train journey, the man in the opposite seat makes a remark that could be the prelude to a conversation. Do you:

   A   Bury your head in your book/newspaper/laptop?

Test

    B Launch immediately into conversation and by the end of the train journey have shown him photos of the kids/the dog/your nearest and dearest you keep on your phone?

    C Respond politely but allow the conversation to peter out?

3 How many of your workmates have been to your home?

    A None.

    B Most of them – you love opening your home to hold parties even for people you don't know well.

    C One or two, with whom you have struck up a friendship.

Those who tend to answer mainly A are intensely private people, maybe bordering on antisocial. Those who go for Bs are on the whole eager puppies in their relationships, friendly, trusting and outgoing. Those who go for Cs are more cautious, willing to be friendly but setting clear boundaries.

While on one level this is no more than a bit of fun, it might be worth taking a moment to consider the implications of your personality type when it comes to deciding how much of yourself you should reveal online. More and more it has become customary to post personal information online. With the rise of Facebook and other social networking sites people are encouraged to share their circumstances and experiences with others, in an open way. There has been much discussion in the media about safety for children online, but remarkably little consideration of what adults should do to safeguard themselves in this relatively new environment. There seems to be an assumption that it is all a matter of common sense, and that unlike children and adolescents, adults are sufficiently clued-up to protect themselves. Indeed, that may be so in most cases.

How the online environment is different

It is nonetheless worth remembering that online can be a very different environment from the real world. Some people think of that as a protection in itself – that they can be whoever they want to be online, and that the anonymity of the internet allows them to be safe.

However, there is one vital difference. The stranger on the train to whom you show your family photographs will probably have forgotten them and most of the conversation an hour after you have alighted at your separate destinations. He certainly will not have access to your mobile to call up the pictures again, nor will others apart from your immediate neighbours on the train have eavesdropped on the interchange.

On the internet, what is posted for others to see may stay there for a very long time. It can easily be transferred to other people, and the person who posted it will not be aware when online pictures or the information are accessed or passed on. What is shared on the internet has a long shelf-life, and it is important to consider this when deciding what to reveal of yourself online. There may even be professional reasons why an individual would deliberately choose not to reveal themselves online, as the next case study shows.

CASE STUDY Dulce Merritt, Psychotherapist, Barbican Counselling

This is a case study about a business woman who, for professional reasons, does not want a personal online presence. She is managing her online image so that she is only found through professional websites rather than on social networking sites.

Dulce Merritt is a psychodynamic psychotherapist working in central London where she runs a counselling practice with four colleagues. Psychotherapists work from different traditions: for example the 'humanist' tradition is an interactive method of working that can allow varying degrees of self-disclosure. Psychotherapists working within a psychodynamic or psychoanalytic tradition, like Dulce, have a long-established process of working where they find value in presenting more of a 'blank canvas' to their clients. So, Dulce's consulting room at Barbican Counselling is plain – it contains books, paintings, a desk and phone, but no photographs. Dulce ensures that the furnishings and setting remain constant. This constancy and the lack of the personal are not accidental, but consistent and appropriate with the professional practice of psychotherapy. The practice has an online presence through its website, **www.barbicancounselling.co.uk**, but the site contains only brief information on the professional qualifications of the individual psychotherapists. Again this is part of Barbican Counselling's carefully considered communications strategy built on the needs of their professional lives.

Dulce explains: 'Some psychotherapists go to considerable lengths to make their canvas incredibly blank. They don't even smile. I personally feel that can come across as cold and maybe even punitive. Every practitioner has to find the balance between being themselves, their personality and an appropriate professional stance.' For Barbican Counselling this means not disclosing personal information. There are sound reasons behind this approach, which can be understood by exploring and valuing what Dulce describes as 'the productive working creative space between the client or patient and the practitioner'. She explains that revealing personal information to the client or patient would be an imposition. This is because psychodynamic psychotherapists allow their clients to use the space as a resource and to fill it with their own thoughts and feelings. In practical terms this also means engaging with the imaginative ideas and questions about the practitioner that are in the mind of the client. The psychotherapist's training gives him or her the expertise to work with these fantasies and ideas and through them to explore the inner thoughts of the client.

'It's because something has gone wrong for them that they have come to talk to me in the first place, and this is one way into their internal world. It reveals how they then structure their existence and how their personality works in interaction with their life. They can't have a completely free fantasy if they know facts about me. And the fantasy is important. You could think of it rather like a dream or a feeling about an event in their life.'

So, the blank canvas is an important element of the work Dulce does with her clients, but like all modern businesses, Barbican Counselling needs an online presence. When looking for a counsellor or psychotherapist, location is an important deciding factor – in London the user will Google 'counselling in London' or 'counselling in the Barbican'. The web is an important tool for the practice and their Barbican Counselling website will appear in postcode searches and geographic searches. But the website has to avoid the personal.

Dulce explains this was not an easy task: 'A website presents a visual image, in a visual medium, but we decided not to have photographs of ourselves. We worked with a designer who is also married to a psychotherapist and understood our needs. So our site gives a sense of place with photographs taken around its location in London and also conveys a feel for what we do. In addition to descriptions of our approach and practical information, there is a picture of water, which is the Barbican lake, but also represents the unconscious, and there is a picture of the statue of dolphins from the Barbican – dolphins represent both happiness and communication in a rather mysterious way.'

Just as the website was the product of considerable planning and care, Dulce has also ensured that any other online information is within her control. Her family would like her to have a Facebook entry: her sister uses Facebook to talk to her children who are at university; two brothers have Facebook sites and post photographs of their families. They have asked Dulce to join them, she has demurred. Her concern is that a new client would be likely to research her background online, and could have access to personal family material and to her family links, which would not be appropriate for her professional work.

'I need to protect my identity, which would be more difficult to control were I on Facebook, even if I restricted access to my page. Photographs could be tagged, for instance. Clients come to see a counsellor or psychotherapist and they care a lot about their own anonymity. You are protecting that as well as offering, through yourself and the work you will do with them, the chance to discover themselves in a new way. They need to be able to model in their mind what they require, and not have to deal with too much of their therapist's personality. Plus, how might they feel about their counsellor's capacity for confidentiality if they also know she is posting personal items on the internet for all to see?'

Dulce's rejection of an online presence is not something she has done without thought and discussion within her practice. She points out that there are a number of famous psychotherapists who have much more of a public persona: many have published academic papers or give lectures.

She cites Mike Brearley, the former chair of the External Relations Coordinating Committee of the British Psychoanalytic Society, as an example of a psychoanalyst who is well established in her own field of work. As former captain of the England cricket team, Mike Brearley uses the fact that he is well known as a tool to explain his thinking. Having captained the England cricket team in 31 of his 39 Test matches, winning 17 and losing only four, he writes and talks on the Art of Captaincy. Duke's view is that, 'You do not have to be totally secretive or anonymous but you just have to be appropriate; the work I do involves thinking about boundaries.'

Online boundaries are an area that she hears about in her consulting room. 'I had a client who told me a Facebook story about updating the status with "Hi I'm available tonight what's happening" and zillions of people responded to her and it suddenly hit her that it didn't feel comfortable.' Dulce's view is that the public/private space is not clearly defined online – people know the online world is public but they still paradoxically insist it has to be private as well. 'I think there is a kind of blindness. It's as if they are wanting to walk naked in the high street and then they are surprised that people are shocked.'

Dulce thinks that the individual should consider more carefully where to draw the line and create boundaries between public and private. Here Dulce recognizes what she calls 'collective learning' in today's teenage generation with a different level of openness in society. But she warns that as situations change in life there are some areas that would be better remaining private – the errors of youth are not appropriate information for business clients: 'I did things when I was a teenager that

I would not want people to know about now – everybody does! I didn't rob any banks but I did stuff like all kids do.' Her conclusion is that just as clients in her counselling practice come to discuss issues of boundaries, so the younger age groups will need to learn online image control and understand the boundaries between public and private.

Online safety tips for adults

It is not difficult to understand why home addresses, telephone numbers and so on should not be published online. But people should also be wary of posting photographs that inadvertently reveal where someone lives. If a house is in any way unique, it can be recognized, especially in conjunction with other information such as the general area in which someone lives. Consider, when posting photographs not only of your own home, but those of friends, that other information may be freely available elsewhere online that would enable someone to pinpoint an address and to combine that with information about a person's movements. Even an innocuous caption to a holiday photo such as 'The family relaxing at our timeshare villa in Italy last July' may have given away more than intended. A would-be burglar might take a guess that since the family were at the timeshare last July, the chances are they will be there again in July this year.

Identify the information you are prepared to allow online

Equally, apparently harmless information released in a personal blog or an 'events' or 'news' column on a website should be carefully weighed to be certain it will not cause problems by revealing too much. An author who posts details on his or her website of forthcoming personal appearances, for instance, is revealing when he or she will be away from home. In itself, this is not an issue, but the author should remember that other information elsewhere on the internet could have rendered him or her more vulnerable than he or she realizes. It is not so much what is revealed in one place, but what the implications are of that information being taken in conjunction with other freely available personal data, that has to be thought through. It is not unusual, for instance, to find an individual using websites such as 192.com that combine information from electoral rolls, telephone directories and other sources. A determined journalist has always been able to track down an address, but now the kind of resources that were once the province only of professionals are available through the internet to everybody.

Pride in one's achievements, coupled with the desire to seem friendly and approachable, has been the downfall of more than one person online. A year or two ago, the about-to-be head of Britain's Secret Intelligence Service, MI6, Sir John

Sawers, received a great deal of unwelcome publicity when it was revealed that his wife had posted family photographs on Facebook. The then British Foreign Secretary denied that security had been compromised, pointing out that the fact Sir John wore Speedo swimming trunks was hardly a state secret. But Lady Sawers had failed to activate privacy controls on her Facebook entry, and had thereby revealed the location of the family's London flat, as well as the whereabouts of the couple's three grown up children and Sir John's parents.

Elsewhere, a disaffected employee decided to share with her friends via Facebook her less-than-complimentary thoughts about her job and her boss. Unfortunately she forgot she had previously invited him to become one of her Facebook 'friends'. Having read the post, he 'invited' her to leave his employ, since the hapless young woman still had two weeks left of her trial period in the job.

The nuts and bolts of successful gatekeeping

These and similar horror stories about the perils of posting online might deter many people from having any sort of online presence. However, it would be foolish to cut oneself off completely from the advantages of being there. Successful gatekeeping is all about being aware of the global scope of the internet and the potential permanency of anything posted there. Understanding the internet's public nature, and not expecting privacy as a default setting, will help people to add to their online profile only the kind of data they are prepared to share with all and sundry.

Think before you post

The secret is to think before you post. Every time you plan to add a picture to your site, or sit down to compose your personal blog, ask yourself whether you would be prepared to share this thought with your worst enemy, or that picture with the creepiest person you know. Double-check privacy controls if you are using a social-networking site, and be prepared for their failure.

Unless you are entirely happy that you.com should be you-naked.com, it is wise to think of your online persona as needing to be guarded by a series of protective filters. In other words, it is sensible to grade information about yourself so that you have a clear idea of what is to be shared by and with immediate family and close friends; what might be seen by a wider circle of acquaintances, possibly including clients and business associates; and what is to be available to everybody, including total strangers.

Know your boundaries

It is vital to know yourself well enough to set your own personal boundaries. As Dulce Merritt points out, 'You do not have to be totally secretive or anonymous but you should be appropriate.' That could mean thinking through how posting anything personal could impact on your professional life. It might seem amusing to post a set of photographs of your (or someone else's) misspent youth – the school football team mooning from the coach windows on a trip to an away match – but consider how your (or their) clients will react to it. Would you really want to take the risk of alienating people who might not share your relaxed attitude or your sense of humour?

As a starter, sit down and compose a list of what information you are prepared to share with the world, then use this checklist:

✔ What impact will sharing that information have on your professional life and your business?

✔ Will it enhance the way clients/customers see you, as a friendly human face in an impersonal online world of commerce?

✔ Do you feel it could adversely affect your relationships with clients?

✔ Will clients respect you more or less if they are able to access your holiday snaps online?

The answers to those questions will depend upon the nature of your business. However, they also depend on your own individual nature – how private or how public you are prepared to be – and it is wise to know yourself before allowing other people to know everything about you.

Closing the door after the horse has bolted: can anything be done to take down damaging or inaccurate information on the internet? It is relatively easy to police your own postings. But a large part of the information on the web about individuals is not necessarily posted by them. People should be alert to how they are portrayed not only on their own website or social networking site, but also to entries posted online by other people.

Sharing photos is common on social networking sites and sometimes, though embarrassment is not necessarily intended, moments better forgotten can resurface. A minor embarrassment or two is probably no bad thing for the soul, as an antidote to hubris, but occasionally there may be good reasons why a seemingly innocent snapshot should not appear – for instance, for a person in a similar role to Dulce's who wishes to preserve his or her anonymity for professional reasons. It might not be a photo – sometimes old friends decide to reminisce about the past's wilder moments, adding such unhelpful information as: 'and old Johnners, who was the instigator of the whole affair and personally draped the lady's underwear over the statue of the founder, is now a High Court judge!'

If the offending item has been posted by a good friend or relation, the obvious remedy is to contact them and ask them to take it down. The friendship may suffer as a result, and you may go down in their estimation as a killjoy, but it might be worth it if you have genuine reason to believe your business or professional reputation will suffer, or if personal information is revealed that might put someone at risk. If you approach them politely, explaining why you are concerned and asking them to imagine themselves in your position, they will probably accede to your request if it is a reasonable one.

It goes without saying that the same understanding is unlikely to be accorded to the famous. Celebrities have to learn to live with embarrassing moments surfacing from their past. Indeed it is more likely that a celebrity who complains will only receive more unwelcome attention, and be pilloried for having no sense of humour. In such cases it is probably better to grit your teeth and ignore the offending picture or anecdote.

But what if the item is not merely professionally embarrassing but also untrue? There are several notorious incidents involving the online encyclopaedia, Wikipedia. In late 2005, the 78-year-old former editor of *The Tennessean* newspaper in the United States, John Seigenthaler, was surprised to discover that not only was he apparently a suspect in the assassinations of both John and Robert Kennedy, he had also lived (without noticing it) in the Soviet Union for 13 years. The information had been posted in his Wikipedia biography as a prank – but it had been online for four months before he knew about it.

The strength of Wikipedia – that it can be edited by anyone – is also its weakness. Since Mr Seigenthaler wrote about his experience in *USA Today*, Wikipedia has been more vigilant, and maliciously false information is often taken down within hours of posting or even within minutes on more high-profile entries. Nevertheless, info-vandals are everywhere online, and it is possible for misinformation about an individual to find its way onto the internet and take root.

This is especially worrying if the information is on Wikipedia, as its entries tend to score relatively highly on search engines, so anyone searching your name via Google, Yahoo or other engines will come across it sooner rather than later. Much of the time its 'mistakes' are a source of mirth and fool no one but the most gullible – the film actress Deborah Kerr, for instance, was reported to have retired from the screen to found a chain of abattoirs. But occasionally misinformation appears that could seriously damage a person's reputation or affect his or her professional life. Politicians tend to complain most loudly about this, although there is evidence to suggest that some of them are not above tampering with Wiki entries themselves.

The Wikipedia entries for some politicians, including Barack Obama, enjoy special 'semi-protected' status so that they cannot be modified by anonymous users. Nevertheless, British politicians David Cameron and Nick Clegg were not accorded that status in the year before they formed the Coalition Government, and during that time visitors to their entries could have come across the untrue claims that Mr Cameron's father had 'bought' him the leadership of the Conservative Party, and that Mr Clegg had slept with 3,000 women and become a member of a hip-hop collective called the Wu Tang Clan.

It is not so difficult to spot that such claims are false, and they were taken down very quickly by Wikipedia's team of volunteer administrators. However, another British politician, Liberal Democrat MP Martin Horwood, found that his entry had been altered in such a way, he believed, as to affect his chances of re-election in a key marginal seat. His immediate impulse was to try to correct the entry himself, but he was warned that this was considered bad form by the administrators and that any changes he made would be removed. It took a great deal of negotiation, and some back-up from technologically literate friends, to arrive at a form of words that the administrators were prepared to allow to correct the perceived bias.

What can be done about online misinformation, be it malicious or an innocent mistake? In the case of Wikipedia entries, the person (or company) that is the subject of the article is not allowed to edit it. Nor is it always a good idea to ask someone else to do it for you. Some years ago, a Microsoft employee objected to what he thought was 'slanted' language in a Wikipedia article on a Microsoft project. Recognizing that it might not look good if Microsoft applied pressure to Wikipedia for the article to be changed, he e-mailed a contact outside the company and asked him if he would be prepared to look at the article and correct it so that it was more objective. But the idea backfired when the contact went public, implying that Microsoft had been trying to use him to manipulate its image.

A better solution is to raise the issue in Wikipedia's own discussion area. If the information about you or your company is demonstrably inaccurate, contact Wikipedia and ask the administrators to take it down. Meanwhile, start an online conversation anywhere you can about what has happened in order to spread the word that you have been the victim of misrepresentation.

It is of course necessary to have discovered the misrepresentation in the first place. Googling oneself is usually seen as vanity. Perhaps it should be seen instead as an essential form of vigilance in an online world where reputations can be made and lost in an instant.

Action to stay in control

- Know yourself.

- Try the test at the start of this chapter.

- Ask yourself the following questions:
  — What impact will sharing that information have on your professional life and your business?
  — Will it enhance the way clients/customers see you, as a friendly human face in an impersonal online world of commerce?
  — Do you feel it could adversely affect your relationships with clients?
  — Will clients respect you more or less if they are able to access your holiday snaps online?

Chapter Five
Getting famous

There are many different reasons why you might want to have a higher profile online. It might be so that you can attract more customers to your business, or sell more of your product. Or perhaps you want to expand your group of friends, or form a group of experts and exchange ideas with them. It might even be that you are dedicated to the Andy Warhol idea of fame for 15 minutes! Whatever the reason you want to become better known through the internet, the digital world will work with you to get your ideas across to new people – and social media is the perfect means but you have to know how to use it.

Social media

Most businesses remain sceptical about social media, and it's certainly true that most corporate communications are usually very dull, even when they have been written by the press team in a friendly manner. Some businesses still dislike the use of Facebook and Twitter and will discourage their staff from using them during office hours – some even block the sites altogether.

More enlightened employers recognize that the social media sphere is an excellent promoter of business ideas and sales leads, and positively encourage their staff to visit the sites. More and more businesses have a Facebook presence, and some management teams believe that soon the Facebook site will be more visited than the corporate website.

For individuals who want to become better known, or even famous, using social media is an excellent method of creating a profile because it is based on conversation and entertainment – and that is the best way of getting traction and resonance with your potential fan base. Because a page on social media is a conversation rather than a promotional leaflet or an article in a newspaper, it is one of the best ways of connecting with people. Once you have one person who thinks you are brilliant then they can become a supporter for your brand or personality.

Any type of business or individual can use social media to create customers or a fan base – if you are a dentist you can have a web cam in your waiting room to show smiling customers coming in and out; if you are a farmer you can show your happy sheep in the fields; if you are an artist you can provide updates on your latest project via social media sites. But how do you begin?

CASE STUDY   Nancy William of Tiger Two

Nancy William's company, Tiger Two, advises individuals
and companies on how to raise their profile online. It has been operating
for five years and focusing predominantly on social media since 2007.
'The thing that I really liked was the idea of blogging,' says Nancy,
'allowing people to write as they wanted, when they wanted, in a public
forum. I thought it would be a good idea to help people and businesses to
get to grips with blogging. And then Twitter sprang up, and Facebook
started to become more mainstream. By the end of 2007 it was pretty
clear that the whole of social media was something which needed to be
looked at.'

At that point, Nancy imagined that her company would concentrate on
online reputation management, a growing field of business in the United
States. But it didn't work out exactly that way. 'To be honest,' she admits,
'most of the people who came to us who wanted their reputation
managed were crooks, people who had something to cover up. Those
weren't the kind of people I wanted to work with – I would rather be
helping people use social media in a positive way, rather than as a way of
burying something awful they did in their past that they didn't want the
world to see.'

Instead, Nancy decided to teach the use of social media – it does include
some advice on how to look after your reputation, though that is not the
core of her business model. Instead the consultancy part of her

organization is about encouraging businesses (and individuals) to develop a strategy for social media, and helping them to implement it. Most of the individuals she works with tend to be within the arts: visual artists, authors and musicians who need to make themselves that little bit more visible than anybody else within a highly competitive field.

Identify your goals

Nancy begins by helping the person she is working with to develop a strategy. 'I always say before you even turn a computer on you need to know where you're headed. So we spend time to work out firstly, what are their goals.'

For an artist this might be to sell more paintings; for an author, to sell more books. For an actor it might be to persuade more people to watch his or her latest TV appearance; for a manufacturer or retailer, it might be to launch a new product line and boost its sales, or for a business such as a garden centre or a dental surgery it might be to encourage more customers through the door. It is important, according to Nancy, to set yourself tangible goals so that you know from the start why you are using social media and what you want to achieve. The purpose of your online activity is to direct followers towards a call to action, which will help you achieve your goal.

From that, other questions flow. 'We ask our clients to consider: who are they trying to reach? Who do they want to speak to? Basic marketing questions. Who is your target audience? Where are those people? What kind of thing are they responding to at the moment? And what kind of thing can this particular individual do to try and capture some of that very rare commodity of attention, which there seems to be less and less of these days with the burgeoning of the internet.'

The right site

By asking such questions, Nancy can help an individual identify which are the *right* sites for them to use. 'People panic: "Oh, there are so many social media sites – how am I supposed to spend time on all of them? I don't have time. What am I going to do?" So we advise limiting it to just one or two where you can get started, the ones which are going to give you the biggest impact.' It might be one of the big sites – LinkedIn, Facebook, and Twitter – but not necessarily. 'Popular opinion is well, as long as you're on Twitter or Facebook, then you're ok. But my argument is that if your audience is not on Twitter or Facebook, there is absolutely no point in being on Twitter or Facebook.'

In other words, it is important to explore first whether there are better ways to reach your particular audience than through the big sites that everybody talks about. 'For musicians, we start looking at sites like My Space, which used to be a social networking site but now is very much music-based. But for authors, there are quite a few booklover social media sites, and of course the audience on those sites are people that adore reading. A writer is better off spending his or her time with a more select group of people who all love to read, than spending time with a very large group of people of whom perhaps only 15 per cent might enjoy reading. So for authors, we suggest they go on to sites like GoodRead or Library Thing. There are also certain blogs, such as one called Red Door aimed specifically at bringing writers and readers together. You get a lot more bang for your buck if you're spending time there rather than just using Twitter or Facebook.'

For a dentist or a cosmetic surgeon, say, the target audience would be patients. Of course there are professional networks for medical people and people within dentistry, but to reach potential patients it is more important to work out where they might be spending time. 'Let's say as a dentist you specialize in children's teeth, for instance,' says Nancy. 'Then you would go somewhere like Mum's Net, a site where you would find mothers who are concerned about their children's health. That would be a much better place to spend your time because you're going to be talking to people who are really important for you in order to build your reputation and your status.'

Develop the blog habit

Nancy usually recommends that people try to develop a blog or a similar regular 'update' their fans can follow. This could sit either on one of the blogspot websites or on your own website if you have one. 'It doesn't have to be a written blog,' she says. 'It could be, say, a podcast if somebody is better at recording their spoken voice. Or it could be a video blog if they want to make short videos.'

This will be your hub – the place where you can put most of your intellectual knowledge, in the form of articles, short clips or audio files. You can use other sites like Twitter and Facebook, or LinkedIn, to drive followers to the hub. But on the hub itself you will have your call to action, where you will ask people to do something that will help you to achieve your goals.

Nancy cites the example of an artist she worked with, through the agent that represented the gallery where his paintings were being shown. 'Ultimately his goal was to get people to come to an exhibition to buy his paintings, so that was the call to action. We used some Facebook advertising and Twitter in order to attract people to the gallery.'

Quality, not quantity

Nancy warns that it is important not to lose sight of your goals and become led astray by how many people you are reaching via social media. 'Too many people become blinded by the numbers. They attract all these friends or followers. But then they just stop and rest on their laurels. They don't realize they actually have to take that group of followers one step further, otherwise they're not going to achieve their goals. Because I could have 100,000 followers – that's great. But if none of them buy my services, then I'm out of business.'

Online press releases

For some clients, Nancy advises the use of online press releases. These work exactly the same as normal press releases except that they are distributed exclusively via the internet, and they are issued to alert the media world of your latest activity.

A press release can work superbly for you, as it can take you beyond online media and bring you to the notice of newspapers, radio or TV. These 'old' mainstream media to some extent still rule the roost. 'No matter how wonderful social media is, the mainstream media still has the biggest effect,' says Nancy. 'We hear people say, "I'll only do social media now, I'm not going to bother with advertising or press releases" – that's actually a pretty poor decision. Because if you get written up in a newspaper, you will achieve much more impact than if you get written up on a blog with perhaps a thousand readers. My own company had a write-up a couple of years back in *The Sunday Times*, and the phones just went mad. We have had a presence on social media for much longer, and although through that we get people calling us relatively regularly, it does not have anything like the same impact we had from the newspaper coverage.'

If you can carry out activity online so that it brings your name to the attention of the mainstream news media, then you will be doubling your impact. However, there are pitfalls, not the least of which is that online press releases can cost you quite a lot of money! For instance, one way of distributing an online press release very effectively is via the news wires, run by companies like Reuters or the Press Association (PA). For an upfront fee the online news wire will arrange to optimize your press release and deliver it to a certain list of journalists. Some companies have a sliding scale of charges, depending on how targeted you want the release to be. 'It depends how much you're willing to spend as to how much notice it's going to get,' says Nancy. 'So you may need deep pockets if you want to distribute your press release in this way.'

However, there are cheaper ways of bringing your online press release to the notice of journalists. 'This is another reason why having your own blog is a good idea,' Nancy advises. 'So that if you create a press release, it can also be put onto your own website or blogspot. A lot of journalists, as well as looking at the news wires, will be doing Google searches. If you've constructed your press release cleverly on your blog, then there's a very good chance that it could be found within a Google search. So you've got two ways then of being reached by mainstream journalists.'

The secret is to optimize your press release so that it contains keywords that your potential audience – journalists or other bloggers – might be searching for. 'If you put your press release out and the title is something like "New Product, Look Here", that really won't help you, because it is not specific enough,' says Nancy. 'But let's imagine our dentist composes a press release titled "New Dentistry Techniques for Toddlers' Teeth". Straightaway, you have keywords there which could be picked up by somebody searching: "dentistry", "toddlers", "teeth".'

So to optimize any written communication you need to think carefully about the kind of words that you use, particularly within the title of your press release. The trick is to get inside the mind of the person that you are trying to reach – what words will they use to search for the information they need? 'That can be easily done by anybody,' Nancy points out. 'And it's really important to be able to put that information out in as many places as possible for people to find it.'

Engage with your followers

Social media is all about the relationship that you create with your followers. Nancy encourages her clients to make individual connections.

'People flock to connect with celebrities via social media because they want to feel they have a genuine relationship. Some celebrities just use social media as another form of advertising. But others, like Stephen Fry for example, are much more approachable. Stephen talks individually with people via Twitter, so you can actually have a conversation with the real Stephen Fry. That makes you think, "Wow. I'm having a 'relationship' with this person. I'm having a conversation with him." Of course, outside social media this would never have happened. But if you start having an individual conversation with someone, immediately they'll buy into you – though obviously it depends *how* you speak to them.'

So if you are polite and friendly in your responses to your fans or followers, without patronizing them, they will value that individual response and it will bind them all the more tightly to you. They will see you as a human being who isn't too grand to engage with ordinary people, who has taken the time to answer them. It's the 21st century equivalent, if you like, of the star encountered in the street who is willing to take a moment to sign an autograph for you. And what works for celebrities also works in business or in sales.

Nancy recounts a great example of this from her own experience: 'Several years back I wrote a blog post about a book that I'd read about social media. I was really impressed by it, so I sang its praises. The next morning I came to my blog and the author of the book had found my post. He'd written a comment to say, "Hi Nancy, thank you very much. It's really good to read that you enjoyed my book. What did you think about this …?" And he sought my opinion on a particular aspect of the subject. I was immensely flattered: the author of this book, which is selling worldwide, has actually found me and spoken to me individually, and it feels almost as if he's a friend. So of course now I've bought every book that he's put out since then!'

Nancy advises people who want to increase their online profile to use the same tactic as that author did, which she calls 'blogger outreach' – chatting with bloggers so that they will be encouraged to write about you, or review your work. It is an especially powerful ploy for those who work in the creative industries.

Develop a schedule

Nancy points out that working with social media has to be done in an organized way. 'For our clients, we work out specific periods within their schedule: perhaps telling them that they need to spend 15 minutes a day on Twitter, write one blog post a week, and approach five other bloggers a month for blogger outreach. Alternatively the schedule might be to send out one press release a month. On top of that we will tell them to spend, say, two sessions a week answering fans on their Facebook Fan page. Every individual we work with requires a slightly different strategy, though all are developed from the same basic template for managing interactions through social media.'

So you need to work out your own online schedule for social media, and stick to it. It is no good only responding when you feel like it; you need to develop a consistent routine. 'It's a myth to say there is such a thing as a social media "campaign",' says Nancy. 'That implies a short blitz – but this has to be an ongoing process. I like to use the example of people offline who employ the tactic of business networking. If you go to the same group week in, week out, you will eventually start to build relationships and it will become apparent who you can work with. But it's only over time that you will start to get more referrals.'

Exactly the same thing happens in social media. But alas, there are plenty of stories of large companies who set up a Facebook page just for a campaign and then drop it after two weeks. This is a waste of time, according to Nancy. 'You have to manage the expectations of your potential audience. People expect the page to go on being there, and once they have become a fan, they want to stay a fan. If you disappoint followers by taking down the page, they will be that little bit more cautious next time that you come out online, because they suspect that, again, you won't bother to stick around.' Even more important, though, a two-week campaign does not allow enough time to develop an ongoing connection with your audience. 'The idea of social media is to build relationships with people: to start conversations, to get involved.'

Nancy has worked with a number of authors who have been very successful in designing and maintaining an online social media strategy. 'They will set up a blog and get feedback from their potential readers before they've even published their book. They might put chapters out, or outline plot strands and ask their followers, "What do you think?" Fans might respond and say, "No, that didn't make sense", etc. This process might go on for as long as a year until the book is published – immediately they have an audience ready and waiting to buy it. But even better, they've established a relationship with these people, by allowing them to feel involved in the process of creating this particular work of art. That's what people want, as customers or audiences: they're looking for a sense of belonging. They want to feel that they are valued by the company or individual with whom they're spending their time, energy and money.'

Is it worth setting up your own niche social network?

Inspired by the example of the sites Nancy has mentioned for booklovers, you might ponder whether it is worth setting up your own equivalent in the area you specialize in, be it gardening, cookery, country music, or whatever. The point of this would be to gather to you others interested in the same subject area. You need to tap into a particular passion or interest in which a large enough group is interested, but which may not be serviced already – or, if it is serviced, perhaps not serviced very well.

But Nancy urges caution. 'Remember, attention is a rare and precious commodity, and it is above all limited. Online, we are being asked to do more and more, to give our attention to ever more sites and networks. But nobody has thought to provide us with more hours in the day to do all these things! The problem with setting up a niche social network is that you're asking people to remove their attention from something that already has it, on to your site. You will have to provide something really special to justify them doing that. Think of all of those Facebook wannabe sites out there – and there are hundreds of them. Do we even remember their names? Do we ever go there? No, because they haven't been able to offer something which provides more than the sites where people are already spending their time and attention.'

So to launch a successful niche site you need to provide something better. But if there are already established sites in the same area, even companies with immense resources can trip up when they try to go one better. 'LibraryThing is a very successful niche social network for booklovers, which has been around for a very long time. Their special offering is that they allow people to catalogue all their books, and share book recommendations, and as a result they have tapped into a strong following, which is why I urge my authors to be on there. There are several similar sites, and not so long ago one of the large book publishing companies decided that they could capitalize on the same idea and set up their own site along the same lines. But they were too late for the party. The site flopped because they weren't offering enough for the several million people signed up to LibraryThing and similar sites to change their loyalties and move across to them.'

With that cautionary example in mind, Nancy advises concentrating your efforts on the existing sites and finding ways to use them to your advantage. 'There are hundreds and thousands of sites out there and it is well nigh impossible for you to come up with something completely different. People do, of course – but it's a lot of hard work and especially if this is not your primary job, you're better off sticking with something that's already established.'

Measuring your success

As Nancy points out, it's only possible to measure how successful you are if you set goals to start with. 'It amazes me that so many people launch themselves on social media without any goals and then declare, "Oh, we're doing so well." My response is: but at what? What exactly was your purpose? I had a conversation with a gentleman the other day who answered, "My purpose is to be better known." I asked him how he quantified that, and he told me that he had a huge number of followers. But the point is, are they actually engaging with you or are they just following you?'

The only way to know for sure is to have set yourself measurable goals right from the beginning. For the artist with the goal of selling paintings, the author who wants to sell more books, or the dentist who wants more patients through the door, it is easy to count success in numerical terms. There are also sites that can help you measure how much reach you've gained on the internet. Even popularity is quantifiable, not in terms of numbers of followers, but by how much you're being talked about and what people are saying. 'Is it positive? Is it negative?' says Nancy. 'You should monitor constantly, keeping in mind *what am I doing this for? What are my ultimate goals? What do I want these people to do? What is the call to action?* That helps you steer your activity in the right direction.'

What advice in a nutshell would Nancy give to anyone wanting to use social media to make themselves better known? 'Ultimately most of us are in business, or creating, or pursuing our own path to celebrity because we want to earn a living from it. You're better off speaking to 100 people who really want to listen to you than 100,000 people who are just racking up their numbers. Goodwill and lots of numbers on Twitter don't pay the rent.'

So, having heard how Nancy advises her clients to get famous via social media, how can you adapt and apply similar techniques to your own activity, and what practical knowledge do you need to do so? In the next section we'll look in particular at how best to use Twitter.

The nuts and bolts of getting famous

Always create a genuine conversation – as Nancy has shown us, people prefer brands and stars who listen to their ideas. You will notice that many big companies have a page where you can ask questions: that's because they have read the research by the Global Web Index that found people think better of brands that provide a page on a social network where you can ask questions.

First consider where you need to be:

- *Facebook* is more than a network for friends; it is used for marketing products, finding new clients and talking to potential customers.

- *Ning* is an online platform for the world's organizers, activists and influencers to create their own social network. It allows you to design a platform to create your own subject-specific network. With more than 300,000 active Ning Networks created across politics, entertainment, small business, non-profits and education you can use the network to connect on the topics you are passionate about.

- *Industry-specific communities* – from law to healthcare, from education to administration there are professional communities online, with specific groups of interest ready for you to join.

- *Twitter* is a social networking and microblogging service that allows you to send short text messages of 140 characters in length, called 'tweets', to your friends, or 'followers'. It will also allow you to answer a question posed by someone else.

Twitter is attractive because you only have a short number of words in each tweet – a great relief compared to reading a massive report or receiving a long e-mail. More important, you can share information with people with whom you wouldn't normally exchange e-mail or instant messages, so you are opening up your circle of contacts to an expanding community. The messages can be sent using the Twitter website, or via a third-party application such as Twirl, Snitter, or the Twitterfox add-on for Firefox.

If someone wants to read your tweets he or she becomes your follower. You have a limit of followers of 2,000 – although this can be lifted to a higher number if you become very popular! The great thing is that it is easy, and it remains simple whatever number of followers you have. Whether you have two followers or 1,000, when you tweet they all receive the same information at the same time. All tweets are indexed, and you can see them at **search.twitter.com**.

Twitterers are often the first to break major news stories by giving instant information from the site of the action. If you want to know something new, then type in the keyword of the subject that interests you and you will be the first to know what is happening.

If you have tweeted a story, the people who are reading it will immediately look at your profile page to see what kind of expert you are – and will also look at other tweets you have created in the past. Your expertise will put your understanding of the action into context. Often the followers will look at other tweets from the same event to see if your views are like everyone else's. Other points are:

- Experienced tweeters are given more credibility than those who are tweeting for the first time.

- If you have just opened your account, your followers are less likely to believe everything you write than if you have been an accurate tweeter for several years.

- A new follower will look at your account and go back to see if you have tweeted about this subject before, and if you connect with other people on this subject.

- It's very important to remember that your past tweets will inform people about your future tweets.

Tweeting and Google

Followers will also have Googled your Twitter name. When you sign up to Twitter it recommends you use your real name; this is because followers are wary of inauthentic or virtual people. You are expected to be real, and to link your tweets to your LinkedIn account or Facebook if you have a page there.

How to talk to a tweeter directly

Your fans or followers may want to send you a direct message (this is done with @reply). This helps them create an idea of what kind of person you are and understand what you are talking about.

Using Twitter to create news

This can work in several contexts – for instance if you have a new piece of information or gossip, or perhaps you are announcing a special sale of products. You can do so very easily via Twitter. Followers are like customers: even if they haven't actually bought from you, they understand that you are trying to sell something special and the reason they are following you is because they are waiting to hear what it is. The more followers you have the more likely it is that one of them will buy something.

Different Twitter accounts

If you work within a company it makes sense for *each individual in that company to have his or her own Twitter account.* This is far preferable to a company tweet, because social media is strategic for personal interactions, each aimed at specialist groups of people. Each individual will attract the people he or she knows are interested in the subject. General information is too dull for Tweeting, so make sure your communications are lively and engaging.

FutureTweets

In normal mode, tweets are sent as soon as you create them. However, a new product, FutureTweets, allows users to schedule tweets to appear in the future. This means you can plan your campaign and which tweet you want to send at a particular point. But you must remember to check your profile each day to see if you have had specific responses, and to answer them!

Finally, remember what Nancy stresses to her clients: social networks are about creating relationships and then maintaining them. You need to draw up a firm schedule for yourself so you never neglect your online commitments. Think of your relationship with your followers as a kind of marriage – as your parents probably told you, making a marriage work *takes* work! And if you put the effort in, the relationships you create will reap you rich rewards.

Action for getting famous

- Write down your goals.

- Who are you trying to reach?

- Who do they want to speak to?

- Who is your target audience?

- Where are those people?

- What kind of thing are they responding to at the moment?

- How can you capture their attention?

Chapter Six
Getting a job

One of the most common reasons people decide to work on their online profile is to help them find work. It might be, if they are self-employed, that being online can help them generate new projects and assignments, by advertising their expertise. Or perhaps they are looking for a job, or a new career in a different company or even a different industry.

The recession has everyone worried. The old-fashioned paper curriculum vitae (or biography or resume), which was once an essential tool in the search for a job, is now out of date. But you still need a CV. In fact online you need lots, but in different formats. This chapter is going to show you how to get the best use out of the business networking sites mentioned in the case study – LinkedIn and Plaxos; how to prepare your biography for job search engines; and some important guidelines for business image management. It will reveal how being online can help you both in a job search and in developing a business network – even if you are already in work and only 'testing the water' to see what else is out there that might suit you.

CASE STUDY Lucinda Craig, jobseeker

Lucinda already has a job, working on a project for a large charity in London. Her field of expertise is market research and over the years she has worked for many different companies and organizations in that capacity. However, although she is not looking for a job immediately, her contract with the charity is due to come to an end next year, so she has decided to keep an eye on the jobs market and put out early feelers by going online.

'I'm just dabbling my feet in the water, to keep abreast of what's available in my field, and the new jargon in my industry,' says Lucinda. 'Because the world of work today is changing all the time. Everything has gone digital. Previously, you might have a specific job spec, or a specific industry to look at. Now all the boundaries between different jobs have changed, and the job opportunities in my area are quite different from the job opportunities two, three or five years ago. Even the name of the kind of position I would be interested in has changed. It used to be called "market research". Then it became "consumer insight" and now I find I've had to start calling it "engagement" – customer engagement, or any sort of engagement, because it doesn't only have to be customers in the commercial sense. So I'm looking at what the growth areas in my industry are such that I can reshape my CV to match the vocabulary of the new landscape.'

Lucinda knows it is vital to keep reformulating your CV in light of what is happening in the world of work and in your own particular industry. 'It's a question of repackaging, to shape my CV to be ahead rather than behind. There have always been lots of people going for a few positions but now that there are even more people competing for even fewer positions, and those choosing candidates from the pile have to skim-read hundreds of applications, it's all about presentation. You have to seem ideal for the new market, not for yesterday's market. So I'm looking at jobs online to understand how to package my skills and experience for the market of 2015.'

To find out what jobs there are, Lucinda has signed up to a number of job websites run by national newspapers: *The Times, The Guardian* and *The Daily Telegraph*, which are the publications in the UK most likely to carry ads for the kind of jobs she would be interested in. By signing up, she receives e-mail alerts every time a new job that matches her criteria is added to the site, so she is able to get early notice before the ads appear in the newspaper.

'With some job sites, the alerts arrive daily, but I can't bear that, and as my job search is not urgent it suits me that instead an update arrives weekly or fortnightly,' she says. 'When you register on the site you state what salary you are looking for, but rather like estate agents (realtors) when you are hunting for a home, the websites will also send you jobs that are paid above or below the limits you set. It can also be tiresome when they send you notice of positions that are completely unsuitable: although I have specified "market research" and "customer insight" and all the other current buzzwords for what I do, I still get sent data analysis jobs and others that are not remotely connected with what I do.'

In fact Lucinda found her present position with the charity from one of these websites. 'I applied the minute the notification came through, and the charity were amazed at how quickly I responded – because the ad hadn't yet appeared in the print edition of the newspaper, they weren't even aware that it had been sent out.' To be the first candidate to respond helps your application stand out, but the other advantage of receiving early notice is that you have plenty of time to prepare your application and think about how to tailor your CV exactly to the requirements of the job.

As well as the big national newspaper job sites, Lucinda is registered with a local site aimed at women in her area of North London who are looking for part-time work to fit in with the requirements of bringing up a young family. 'It's called Women Like Us, and aimed at mums basically who want a job that's 9 to 3, and close to home so they can be in time for the school run. Most of the jobs are low paid, and a lot are in the charity and public sector. But many sound interesting and stimulating – I probably won't take one of those though because my personal circumstances are moving on from that. But the site is warm and personal, and all bright pink because it's aimed at women, and I love looking at it because sometimes I daydream about doing a part-time job working for a friendly little publishing company just up the road.'

In the past Lucinda has worked in the health industry, so when the time comes to look more seriously for a new job she also intends to register with sites that specifically list jobs in that field. She believes in being proactive and getting your name and CV out there. She also uses the job sites to help her identify particular companies she would like to work for.

'Even if they are not advertising a job at the moment, if I think they might be looking for someone with my skills, I will contact them directly saying I'd like to work for your company. Of course when the time comes I will be applying through the usual channels for jobs too, but I also think it is a good idea to make a speculative application to a company you like the look of. I would like a job tailored to me rather than just a standard post that they're waiting to fill.' Indeed, by planning ahead and getting her profile online already, Lucinda is laying the groundwork to make her next career move a real success.

She also uses LinkedIn, the business networking site, to make sure her name is seen in the right places. However, she sounds a note of warning: you should not expect that simply by being on a site like LinkedIn the networks you join there will miraculously sort out a new job for you. It is better to use it as an individual strand in an overall strategy, so that prospective employers can see you have a high online profile.

'Often, in my particular group of contacts, the same five people are constantly on it,' says Lucinda. 'For one of them, it appears his business is no more than endlessly networking! He's worked for several start-ups and he always does his recruitment through searching around individually, via a very extensive network. But every day he seems to add three new contacts, and publishes dull stuff about whatever conference he's been to. Or another person constantly tweets about the product her company makes, four or five tweets a day, all appearing on LinkedIn, which doesn't interest me either. But in the end, LinkedIn is just a tool. It's a very useful site to register with, but I think you need to be careful how, and how much, you use it.'

It's never too early to start looking

Like Lucinda, if you are thinking of a career move in the future, it's a good idea to start planning sooner rather than later:

- Keep your CV up to date so that it reflects the kind of skills and talents the job market is looking for today.

- Tailor it to suit the specific job you are applying for, and constantly rework it so that it feels fresh and clued-up to the reality of your field or industry today.

- Register with general job sites like the ones Lucinda uses, such as national newspapers.

- Look on geographically local sites too, especially those that specialize in jobs for people with your particular requirements, such as the online site for working mothers in North London that Lucinda found.

- Look for industry-specific job sites to suit your field of expertise.

- Seek out companies you want to work for and be proactive – let them know you are interested in finding a position with them.

- Make contacts with other people in your field via LinkedIn and other networking sites – you never know when their help might be useful to point you in the right direction. It is always much easier making an approach to a company if you know the name of, and better still have networked with, someone there.

- Register with online agents specific to your profession or industry, and upload your CV to their sites.

Without a doubt, having an existing online profile helps you find a job. The sooner you start looking around at what's available, the better you will be able to keep up to date with the ever-changing job market and the more you will understand how to give yourself an edge over other applicants. If you make sure you are present on the right sites, you could even find yourself in the enviable position of having someone approach you with a job offer!

So how do headhunters use the internet to search out the right candidate for the job? The next case study deals with this issue.

CASE STUDY Gill Carrick, headhunter

Gill Carrick is a partner of the international executive
search firm Odgers Berndtson. She is a headhunter who concentrates
largely on media, culture, leisure and entertainment projects at board
level, including the appointment of external directors and public affairs
specialists. In her spare time she runs marathons – New York, London,
Paris – and she is planning more.

Headhunting is built on similar skills to marathon running: it requires
diligence and dedication, and is a very long process. At the start of an
executive search Gill will use the Odgers Berndtson team of researchers
to analyse companies worldwide. If she is looking for somebody to run a
£500 million turnover business, it will provide her with information about
everybody who is running a business of that size, and show their track
record through filed company accounts. At this point, Gill turns to the
internet to find out more. Her research technique involves both online
information and careful study of the individual's track record using the
net as, in her words, 'a wonderful filing cabinet'.

'If I'm appointing somebody to a position of trust, be it a Chief Executive
role in a quoted company, or to run a museum or a gallery, it's essential to
be sure of their ability to perform in that role. You can validate their track
record via a number of sources online.' She uses the internet to check
company results and search for press comments, at the same time as
she talks to people who have worked with the individual. 'The internet

research forms part of my putting the jigsaw puzzle together with regard to people. I need to build up the full picture: that's what the clients are paying for.'

One of the essential uses of online information for executive search is to set the individual in context. Gill may have a candidate who has been exceptionally successful in an organization, but she will look at the economic context of the business success in order to understand if the organization was already successful before the candidate arrived, or if it was the candidate that created the business success.

Just as she is sceptical of success, she is not put off by failure. She approves of the US job market, which is more forgiving of failure than Europe. 'It is better to look at people who have made errors and understand what "mistake" looks like, because they are probably going to be stronger in the future as a Chief Executive. The danger of appointing the person that hasn't made a mistake is that they are always about to make one.'

In the main, Gill doesn't look at social networking sites like Facebook because the senior executives that she places in business roles are unlikely to be members of online social communities. (So rapid is the growth of social media that this may soon change though!) However, she uses business community sites like LinkedIn and Plaxos to find people if she has not been able to track them through personal contacts. She reads the biographies that appear on the business sites, but she maintains: 'Everybody glosses.' Within executive search she conducts rigorous checks to make sure that the biography given to a client is absolutely accurate and that the individual has not misrepresented his or her career.

Perhaps the most useful aspect of online information is its ability to provide what Gill calls a '10-year *Daily Mail* test'. This is a light-hearted reference to an English tabloid newspaper that takes a high moral tone and exposes personal (mis)behaviour. Gill investigates 10 years of press comments to make sure that there are no embarrassing moments in the history of a candidate. She uses an example of a candidate who allegedly couldn't keep his trousers round his waist and had been exposed in many newspapers for affairs with members of his staff. She commented: 'The man had done nothing wrong commercially, but he had ditched the wife and misbehaved badly with a member of his team. The ability to go online and research back 10 years enabled me to delve below the surface of his background.'

She had a similar case where she discovered that her candidate was a recovering alcoholic. 'I tossed it over in my mind as to whether I should reveal this to the client, and in the end I did. I said to the client, this individual has not been convicted of a crime – it's a crime against himself – but possibly you need to know.' Fortunately for the candidate, Gill's background checking also enabled her to give a complete assurance that her man had been dry for 10 years, and so he was appointed to the job.

Gill has found the net a better research tool than using contacts or sources, who are not always willing to remind you of past problems with their close colleagues. 'Having the archive is a good thing from our point of view; it may not necessarily be a good thing from the individual's point of view.' This leads Gill to 'counsel wisdom when it comes to what you post online'. However, she is surprisingly relaxed about young people and their online behaviour: 'You're allowed the sins of youth. You have three or four years to sow your wild oats, and then you need to buckle down.' She says: 'If I was running somebody for a Chief Executive job and I discovered that there were horrendous entries on Facebook, or equivalent, in their history, would that influence us in terms of our judgement? I don't think so.'

But there are occasions when Gill is headhunting for creative functions – director of programmes, or director of content – where she will be more alert to 'sex, drugs, rock n roll' to make sure that it does not undermine the individual's ability to do the job. 'The last thing you want is to put someone in a job without checking properly, only to have the organization ring up six months later and say: "Did you know about the coke habit?"'

The headhunter's job is to look at content online purely in terms of the hard history of the career of the candidate. So the online profile *is* important, in that it is a working track record, but Gill has a proviso: 'Profile is fine and updates are fine, but if you are going to be a media hound it can work against you. It starts to look like this guy is more about creating his own brand than he is about doing the job that he's being paid to do. I would be a little cynical and think: "Oh right, big ego – we need to do some sensible checking on this individual".'

Interestingly, many of Gill Carrick's clients, when asked what characteristics they are looking for, request 'Somebody who is relatively ego-free.' Gill's view is that if somebody is appearing regularly in the press or online, with a constant stream of 'me, me, me' she wants to check them very thoroughly. The headhunter's view of a serious commercial player is that he or she will act with restraint. On the other hand, she is interested in what people are doing online in relation to the job, because it is actions that create the personal brand.

So to build a career, you need judicious use of online press, together with reports on your activities within the organization or your speeches at conferences, but if you want to make your mark with the headhunter you should not overdo it. 'Talk is cheap, as my mum used to say, but actions endorsing your brand, your positioning are really what you want to achieve. There are a myriad of ways in which to build your brand, but choose your brand-building exercises judiciously.'

The nuts and bolts for job hunters

As Gill suggests, looking for the perfect job is a marathon run, not a sprint. Just because you can put your biography online with ease and speed does not mean that you will get a job tomorrow. But the main lesson to take away from Gill's case study is that you need to manage your career image online. If you are going to climb the ladder to success and be headhunted as a chief executive, then you will need a consistent story about your working career.

Where to look for a job online

The most obvious place to look for a job is on the website of the organization where you would like to work. Many larger companies have RSS feeds that alert you to jobs that come up on their site.

Most of the headhunters or agents advertise searches that they are working on, so you should check their sites and register with those that are appropriate to your training and background. There are job sites that advertise jobs where you select what you are looking for with a search focus on location and salary. Many of these job sites will e-mail you when a job with the search characteristics you have listed is posted and, as Lucinda explained, even if you are happily employed it does no harm to register with job sites so that you know what prospects are 'out there' and are ready for a move when the time comes for promotion.

Filling in forms online

Whatever online business networking site you choose, you will have to fill in its information form in the format it provides. It is easier to compare biographies when the format is the same, so many employers insist on digital application forms to make the process easier for them. Unfortunately there is no quick solution here, and each application form will take as long to write – more marathon training for the job applicant! The key tip here is to start the process early. Many jobs have a deadline for the application, and you do not want to leave it till the last moment and be sending your form at midnight, as that will be the one time that your broadband line collapses, or your computer freezes.

Let's assume you have a biography already written in Word format on your computer. It will be written in the first or third person. It will not exaggerate your successes nor will it mention things you are bad at. First thing is to spell-check and then fact-check your information. Then, if you copy and paste the material into a format, you are certain it will be correct.

Online forms are a nightmare – much longer and more detailed than a paper CV. If you are used to writing short e-mails online remember that this is a job application and abbreviations and a relaxed style may not be what the employer is looking for – it is easy to be misinterpreted online so keep your answers formal. It makes sense to copy the headlines of the format you are using and then draft your replies in Word before you drop them into the format box. Annoyingly, not all formats allow you to cut and paste, so check before you start so you know how long it will take you to complete the task.

When you have completed the form make sure the dates of your previous jobs are coherent, that you have given the correct phone number and the e-mail address is accurate. Before you send off the form, print out a copy so that if you are lucky enough to get an interview you can remember what you wrote. You should have tailored your biography to match what the job requires, and you will need to refer back to what you wrote.

Business networking

Registering with one of the business networking sites mentioned by Gill – Plaxos or LinkedIn – is a useful way of keeping a permanent profile online and making contacts that will be helpful in your professional life, whether or not you are seeking a job.

LinkedIn is an online business card network site with almost three-quarters of its users college graduates. It is one of the older social networking sites and already has a slightly old-fashioned feel to it, partly because the user has no layout control and you cannot create your own design. To date it has no applications – you cannot exchange gifts or videos, there are no sounds and you can't buy virtual potted plants or other embellishments to add to your home page. But its good points are simplicity and an easy-to-use layout.

Warning – if you are new to LinkedIn you can use your Outlook address book to upload your contact list, and it will automatically invite people to contact you. This is a process you need to do with care and consideration! Your Outlook address book may contain contacts that have never heard of LinkedIn (your aunt perhaps) or even more embarrassing, the address of a chief executive whom you hardly know and would not expect to connect with. Avoid the 'contact everyone' button, or you will find you have sent invitations to people who will find your request perplexing, embarrassing or downright annoying.

Value for money

LinkedIn is an excellent way of connecting with people you don't know, and if you are looking for employment you are going to be networking with new business contacts. If you are planning to send your CV to someone you can find information using a company search, and on an individual basis you can find out about the person and their previous jobs. The price of a business message to someone you don't know is US$5 – a very good investment because 30 per cent of respondents reply, a much higher response rate than an average e-mail.

Imagine that you want to set up a meeting with someone from the marketing team at a large organization – type in the organization name, find the person you think might help you, and send them an e-mail. LinkedIn has a straightforward 'advanced search' so you can find people by company name, address or state, or industry groups. You can find people you know but haven't yet linked to by looking at the 'other connections' of your linked colleagues, and link to them on your network. Group connections are free, so it is possible to join an old business school group or marketing group that could come in handy for job applications.

Similar to other networks, if you want to make it work for you then you need to put in time. Remember, this is a marathon, not a sprint. You need to spend time every day on the site (even if it's just a few minutes) to ensure you are part of the community.

Using LinkedIn

Like all networking sites, you should upload a photograph to create interest in your profile. Make sure that all your details and dates are accurate. Gill cynically believes that all users are likely to 'gloss' their biography, but if you are planning to link to people you are working with, or once worked with, it makes sense to stick to the real facts. Your former colleagues will know the truth about your role and title.

The site does not allow people to ask for an e-mail address without knowing the person. But if you are happy to make your e-mail available to all users, then use your e-mail address as a handle to your last name, then anyone who finds you interesting can contact you directly.

As with other social networking sites, whenever you update your profile the information will be sent to those who are connected to you. If you use one of the LinkedIn affiliated organizations such as Word Press or Slide Share, you can feed content from your blog to the LinkedIn profile, and it will be updated whenever you update the blog on Word Press or a presentation on Slide Share.

LinkedIn gives you a formal process for connecting with people, but it allows you to customize the message with your own words. It makes sense to use this, and to personalize all messages, as well as creating personal recommendations for other people. If you do this, other people will recommend you, and their recommendation will be on the front of your profile page.

Reputation building

LinkedIn also offers a useful reputation-building process by allowing you to join groups related to your subject interest. Once a member, you can ask questions of the group or start discussion threads. If you answer a group question, then everyone can read your thoughts on the topic and you are building your profile as an expert, not least because when you answer the question your name and career summary are given. Click at the top of the group page to get an RSS feed of the new questions. If you want, you can invite new members to the group.

Like any other network you have to be part of it – so if you are looking for a job you should expect to spend a few minutes every day on the site making sure you are part of the community.

LinkedIn summary

These are the simple tricks that will help maximize your profile on LinkedIn:

- Upload a decent photo (make sure you look business-like; this is not a dating site).

- If you meet someone new and would like to ask them to link to you using the invitation control panel, use the formal note provided but add a careful, personalized note yourself such as, 'It was good to meet you at the seminar – let's talk.'

- Use your e-mail address or Twitter handle as an adjunct to your last name. On LinkedIn you can't get people's e-mail without knowing them already so giving your e-mail makes certain that they can contact you immediately.

- Use keywords liberally. The profile you create will be scanned by the Google search engines, so if you are looking for a specific job, for instance in marketing, add the word 'marketing' to your profile, and any other keywords that will help lift you to the top of a search.

- Make sure you use similar keywords for your website and blog. Remember that people can subscribe to your blog from LinkedIn.

- Make sure you opt in for the update status so that whenever you update your blog or twitter account, the information will be distributed to those who are connected to you on LinkedIn.

- Similarly, ensure that applications that you have created directly are fed back to your LinkedIn profile. If you have created a slide in Slide Share you can link it back to your profile, so all your contacts can look at your new work.

- Look at the connections of people you know but haven't yet linked to; look at connections of your good friends and link to them; browse to the 'other connections' of your friends and colleagues and link to them on your network.

- LinkedIn has a clever search – you can find people by company name, zip code and industry groups.

- Develop the 'recommendations' element of LinkedIn. When you ask people to recommend you, give them an idea of the area in which you are looking for work, and what skills you would like recommended. This will help others know what your skill base is.

- Use the internal messaging – the private e-mail system within LinkedIn uses messages to send to your connections. You can send 50 messages to your designated connections on the regular LinkedIn membership.

- Build your reputation by using LinkedIn Answers. This is a collection of different topics where LinkedIn members ask questions and answer them – you can get an RSS feed of all the new questions and do a quick scan of all questions that day. If you can answer any of them, you could have your name built into a profile as 'best answer' in the category. This is free publicity for your skill: when you answer a question, your name and address will be attached to it along with a summary of what you do.

- LinkedIn Groups is a major feature of the site, so consider making your own group and invite members to join you; that way you can build your own professional network.

Business image management guidelines

However hard you try to separate your personal and professional life online, it is going to be difficult to disconnect them. You will have seen in the case study that the top headhunters look at your personal and professional life when considering you for a job. Don't panic. Your personal life is not under scrutiny in all job applications. Gill Carrick was looking for chief executives, many of them at the high point of their careers. If you are just starting out, you may not face the same scrutiny – intelligent headhunters know that wild behaviour in your 20s is to be expected.

However, your online image will be considered in the context of your own generation. Older people have the advantage that they sowed their wild oats at a time before the internet laid everything open to public scrutiny. They can sometimes get away with denying allegations. But if you are in your late 20s or younger, it is unlikely that you will be able to cover up your vices. The probability is that there exists a phone-photo record of misdemeanours stored on Facebook or someone's hard drive. I doubt there is a single young person in their final year at university (apart from the nerdy ones) who doesn't possess incriminating photos of someone else, given that everyone has digital cameras these days, so consequently, and damningly, younger people today will have their teens and early 20s more documented than the older jobseeker.

On the other hand, perhaps society will gradually have to change its norms with regards to these images. It will be ridiculous if, come 2025, it is considered a major scandal if photos surface of a public figure enjoying a drink or not wearing many clothes. There will be incriminating material on most of tomorrow's leaders available on a memory stick somewhere. But for the moment, beware of gaffes that could cause you future embarrassment, especially if like many young people you've indulged in 'sexting' – the use of new technology to send explicit messages with photographs from phone to phone. Often the originators are women, so no doubt there will be quite a few female public figures of tomorrow who will have 'sexting' come back to haunt them.

Online, your personal and professional lives are ever more connected. Thus it makes sense to avoid writing or posting anything that would compromise your ability to get a job. Many websites have privacy tools, but you should assume that they do not work. Everything you send or receive from a social networking site is public. When the privacy settings change and are strengthened, you can assume that the previous settings were not adequate.

It is important to check which details appear live and which are part of your registration process. The networking site Plaxos has its focus on business connections, and suggests you share work contact details and phone numbers. A number of high profile users have removed their details because any user logged on can see their details. With other social networking sites such as Facebook and LinkedIn, only people whom a user has agreed to view (in some way or another) can view certain parts of that user's profile. This highlights the need for anyone with an online profile to know exactly what information they are sharing with others and to be aware of who is following them online.

Learn how to remove as well as set up your business networking profile

Although you can close a social networking site, the cache of the site will remain online (and searchable to those with technological skills). So if you have a risky profile on a social site, removing it is not the final answer. Indeed removing the account might be harder than you first think. For example it is easy inadvertently to open a duplicate site on LinkedIn and when you try to close the account you are sent the message 'it may take a few days to close the account'. It would be better not to have opened the account to start with.

To close a LinkedIn account, this is what you do:

Go to Accounts and Settings (in the top bar).

Under Settings, look under Personal (a column in the right-hand side).

Fourth heading down is Close My Account.

Finally, always ensure you have a consistent story about your working career and never write anything online that would compromise your ability to be employed. However good the privacy tools of the website appear to be, it is better to assume they do not work.

Action for jobseekers

- Research job opportunities with a wide perspective, knowing that all the boundaries between different jobs have changed.

- Tailor your CV to suit the specific job you are applying for, and constantly rework it so that it feels fresh.

- Give yourself plenty of time – job seeking is a marathon, not a sprint.

- Use LinkedIn with care as it can upload your entire contact list and will automatically invite people to contact you.

- Expect that your personal and professional life online will be connected.

- Learn how to remove as well as set up your business networking profile.

Chapter Seven
Getting your name
in search engines

Before you read this chapter, now is a good time to search for your name using Google, Bing and any other search engine to see what comes up on the first page of the results. Ideally there is a connection to your web page or your blog, but if the result is not what you expect then this chapter will show you how to ensure that under your name is the information about you. The theory behind Google's search engine (and Google is the established leader in the field of search) is that the first page of results will be the closest to what the average person who types in your name is looking for. This strength of relevance to its search words is why Google outshines its competitors.

This chapter explains how you can use the Google search engine to improve the page ranking for your name and take people who are searching for your name to your website or your blog.

What is PageRank?

The mission behind Google is 'to organize the world's information and make it universally accessible and useful'. Like other search engines Google has a process that decides whether a page is relevant – the most appropriate one to meet the search name that you're typing in – by how many other people link to it. It works by assuming that if your page or website has a lot of people linking to it from other web pages then it will contain interesting material. This is a concept called 'PageRank', which works out the quality and appropriateness of any web page based on how many other people link to it.

PageRank is based on an algorithm – a mathematical process that, following a search, determines which page shows up first, second, third and so on. Google describes it as interpreting 'a link from Page A to Page B as a vote, by Page A for Page B'. In other words, a PageRank comes from 'balloting' all the pages on the web about how important a particular page is. A page with a higher PageRank is considered to be more important and is more likely to be listed above a page with a lower PageRank.

However, Google doesn't just look at the sheer number of links a page receives. It also analyses the page that casts the vote, so that votes cast by higher ranking pages count for more and help to make other pages 'important'. There are many other factors that influence PageRank but Google keeps a lot of them under wraps. It's completely automated so there are no humans involved in the ranking mechanism.

How the spider works

Google uses a web crawler (also known as a spider), which it calls Googlebot, to find and fetch web pages that are stored in Google's vast database. Googlebot consists of many computers requesting and fetching thousands of different pages simultaneously. These pages are scanned for hyperlinks that provide new documents to be fetched and stored in the same way. All the words (except for common words such as 'the', 'is', 'or') on these pages are indexed so that when a search is entered the search words can be located in the enormous index and pages containing those words identified. That's when PageRank comes in to rank the pages in order of relevance. Google runs a network of thousands of low-cost computers (one of the things that helped it get so big is that it is very good at building cheap, efficient computers) and can therefore carry out very fast data processing. If you want to know more about this have a look at **www.Googleguide.com/Google_works.html**, an online tutorial not affiliated to Google itself.

So what happened when you Googled your own name? Read next about the Adamson family experience.

CASE STUDY Jonathan Adamson

Jon is a charming and easygoing film director with an international career, working on both sides of the Atlantic. His expertise is in TV drama, where he is known for his excellent direction of lighting camerawork. More recently he has developed skills in 3D film making and is in considerable demand for work on 3D movies.

Jon has a career he loves, and a steady income to support his wife and family. While he travels the world, his wife Suzie is at home looking after their three boys whose ages range from 6 to 13. As you might imagine family life is quite chaotic; the boys are very sporty and spend a lot of time playing soccer. 'It's increasingly difficult,' Suzie says, 'to persuade the boys to do any academic work, as they want to spend their time on the games fields. I have been very worried that if they just play sport they will fall behind with the school work and then do badly in public examinations.'

Suzie knew that her best chance of getting the boys to concentrate on academic as well as sporting activities was to ensure that they went to an excellent school. In her neighbourhood there was only one school that she felt would suit all three boys. She remembers how nervous she was when she filled in the application forms and submitted them to the school: 'I filled the forms in online because my handwriting is very poor and I wanted to make a good impression – as parents we had to fill in our professions and then add any details about the boys that were relevant such as their sporting achievements or musical skills …. Not that they have any musical skills! It's just soccer, soccer, soccer in our house!'

The next step in the school's admission process was an academic assessment. Well that's what the school called it; the boys described it as 'a really difficult exam'. As the day of this test approached, the boys were a little nervous, but Suzie was confident that they would do well. Sure enough, she was right to be optimistic, and the whole family were invited to the school for a final meeting with the headmistress and staff. At this point Suzie was relaxed. 'At last,' she admits, 'I felt confident that the boys were going to be accepted at Headington. After all they are lovely individuals, and with a bit of tutoring they had jumped through the academic hoop. What could go wrong?'

Jonathan came back from a shoot on the East coast to attend the school meeting. He was keen to meet the teachers, and in particular to get to know the headmistress who had an excellent reputation for making the school a leading institution in both sport and intellectual studies. The parents were invited to join the headmistress in her study for a more informal conversation over tea and coffee.

'I'll never forget the moment,' said Suzie, 'when we walked into the large wood-panelled office and were handed bone china teacups, and sophisticated ginger biscuits. The headmistress was working her way around the room and talking to each of the parents in turn. She was asking friendly questions and shaking the hands of the parents. Eventually she made her way to the side of the tea area where Jon and I were standing. I introduced myself, and then introduced Jon. It was at that moment that I realized we had a problem.'

The headmistresses smiling, relaxed face had turned thunderous. She fixed Jon with a freezing glare as he stretched out his hand to shake hers. 'I don't think we have met before,' she said coldly. 'Am I right to think that you are … you are a … (the headmistress was searching for the word she needed) … a film director?' Jon gave his normal friendly grin: 'Oh yes, I make movies' he replied. But as he spoke she grimaced and moved away as fast as possible. Jon had clearly upset her, and the parents' session was over before Suzie had time to find out why.

The following Monday Suzie called the school admissions office and asked if there was a problem with their admissions process. After a few embarrassed moments the secretary said that the admission executive would return the call in a short while. Perplexed, Suzie waited to find out what had gone wrong. How had Jon upset the headmistress? It only took a moment for the problem to be explained. Before the meeting the headmistress had checked the background of each of the parents on Google – what were they best known for? Had they written a book? Had they contributed to charity works? When Jon's name was Googled it was clear he was not a suitable parent. He was a film director, but the Jonathan Adamson whose name was at the top of the list was known for his pornographic movies. Suzie was horrified when she Googled Jon for herself and discovered the same information. Of course her husband made TV movies, not pornography, but that's not what appeared when you typed his name in the search engine.

Needless to say, the mistake was rectified. Jon's TV credits were sent to the headmistress, and the boys were accepted at the school. But had there been other confusions in the past? Jon will never know if he has been turned down for work because of the 'other Jon' who is a pornographer. But what should he have done to ensure that the mix-up never happened to start with?

Nuts and bolts of search engine optimization

When you type you name into Google you have a results page. Google wants to make sure that people can find the information they are looking for as easily as possible and to provide the best possible experience for all the people who use its website. Nobody knows for sure what process it uses – and the process is always changing. The leading search engines do not disclose the algorithms they use to rank pages, but they have a large number of different algorithms that they use to bring to the top the most relevant page for the search words you have used. What we know for sure is that the search results are personalized to each user and their history of previous searches, and the search gives extra value to up-to-date and new information. The key thing to understand is that you will be wasting your time if you try to 'trick' the system into making your name and associated web material come to the top of the search. A much better use of your energy is to make your information the best and most useful in its field. So Jon in our case study should have had his own website with all the detail and information about the movies he was making and had made.

The website

If you want to get to the top of the search engines, when you plan a website you need to choose a good address – or to use its technical term a 'domain name', which will be part of your web address or, to give it the technical term, URL – Universal Resource Locator.

There are two possible approaches to choosing a name. You could be simply descriptive: myname.co.uk or what you do: **myjob.com**. For example, if Jon wanted more work as a film director he could have had his web address as **www.awardwinningmovies.com**, or **www.usafilmdirector.com** would help him find work in the United States. Of course many of the good names have already been taken, but Jon could have come up with ideas based on the TV shows he had directed and added some adjectives – **classicmoviedirector.com**, which would have made his website more distinctive, or he might have mixed his expertise with his name – **TVmoviesfromJonAdamson.com**. The place to find out what names are available, and to buy the one you want, is through one of the many domain name hosting companies. If you visit one of their websites you will find the tools to check whether the name you want is available. If it is, you can then buy the right for a year or more to use that name, at a cost of only a few pounds. At the end of the year you will be asked if you want to renew the domain name. As the cost is rarely very high, it is often worth hanging on to a good domain name especially if it includes using your own name.

Both the .com and .co.uk suffixes – the bit that goes at the end of your URL or web address – indicate that the site is going to be primarily in English, though in theory you could build the site in any language you like. So if you choose one of these, the majority of the people who find your site will be English-speaking.

The preferred suffix for businesses used to be .com because it was among the first to exist (and thus suggested you had been trading on the web from the early days). However, there are now plenty of suffixes to choose from. Some carry more specialist meanings: .org suggests non-profit making organizations and charities, .tv for TV companies, .edu for schools, .ac.uk for British universities. Less specifically, you might also consider .info and .net.

The home page

The home page of the website is usually the most important, and it should say what is included in the site. All the other pages should have a title using the keywords as necessary, and you can 'tag' your titles to other pages. This is important because the search engine 'spider' will look at the name of your home page and the title page tag, which should be relevant to the content of the page. Just be warned that there is no point in giving a tag that is not relevant to the material on the page – by writing 'free chocolate here' when in fact you are a TV director, you will not find more hits to your website – the opposite: you will be dropped down the page rank.

Website structure

If you are setting up your website from scratch you need to be aware that the search engines will look at the structure of your site (known as its navigation system) to see how the internal pages link to each other. Each link should contain a keyword and of course you will set up links to other activities such as blogs and forums that you contribute to. If your website has been developed from a template, then check that the title and the page tags are not the same. Make sure that each page tag reflects the content of the website page.

Keywords

There is no point in endlessly repeating keywords on the website. It is helpful to have them in the headline (Jon might have had 'Director TV movies') but not every other line. So what keywords could you use to lift your name and job higher in the page rank? This is the moment to think about locating the right keywords, honing them, and discovering the exact words that will bring people to your website.

When considering keywords your aim has to be to gather all the words you can think of that someone who wants to find you might type into Google. One way might be to use 'your name' in combination with all the different ways people might describe you: 'TV movies', 'TV films', 'movie director', 'soccer dad' and so on. You are trying to match more specific searches – searches that are likely to result in your website being found.

If you're really smart you may be able to find a little niche area that no one has thought of that doesn't contain your main keyword, whether that's film or TV. You might include a keyword for '3D movies'. The advantage of finding niche words is that other companies might not think of using them but people searching for you will!

Slowly, you can expand your keywords in this way and eventually graduate to using three- or four-word keyword combinations that when they type into the search engine will find you and no one else. For example:

Keyword: Jon Adamson Movie Director – Because Jon has a common name this is very general and unlikely to result in our Jon being found.

Keyword: Jon Adamson TV Movie Director – This is better. It's more specific and shows that the searcher has a little more idea about what they're after.

Keyword: Jon Adamson USA TV Movies – Now we're getting somewhere. What you have here is someone *who we know*.

Keyword: Classic and 3D Movies Jon Adamson – Thinking up all these keywords may sound a little tough. It's not. You don't need to sit there for hours racking your brain for all the different variations that fit who you are and what you do.

You can get help from Word Tracker, which helps you to understand the kind of volume of searches particular words receive. For instance, you might discover that the word 'movie' is receiving 37 million global searches, with around two-thirds of them in the United States, while 'TV movie' is getting just 90,000 searches. Once more, it's clear that being specific pays dividends. Another site worth visiting is Keyword Discovery, which can help you research words that perform successfully and can suggest alternative terms or phrases you may not have considered.

Google will help. If you have an 'ad words' account click the 'Keyword Tool' button and type in your first keyword. This helpful tool will immediately report back to you with all kinds of synonyms and variations and similar words that people may type into a search engine.

Links

Don't link to everything; choose your links with care. A link from your website to somewhere else is only useful if it is a quality link – in other words if the content on the site you are linking to is relevant to people visiting your site. If the site you link to is of high quality with many visitors then you gain ranking from their success. You might want to join a Link Exchange – a group of websites under one head that runs the exchange of links that are inserted into the web pages, but you need to check the group is a true match to your vision and values.

Patience

Don't expect that you are going to make your website at the top of the search engines page ranking immediately – it takes time and patience. If you have built your site around your vision and values and are passionate about it, then you can keep going at making improvements and enjoy what you are doing as you do it.

Action for search engine optimization

- Search results are personalized to each user depending on their history of previous searches.

- Create new information: the search gives extra value to up-to-date entries.

- Make your information the best and most useful in its field.

- Choose your links with care.

Chapter Eight
Getting a result

What is it that you feel passionately about? Other people will feel just as strongly as you do about animal welfare, endangered species, the environment, health, or human rights: it is just a matter of making contact with them.

As we have seen, social networking online can help you achieve pretty much anything you want. By building a profile for yourself online you can make new friends and contacts in both your personal and professional life, keep informed, make a name for yourself, and build a successful career. You can also use it to help achieve a result for other people too, by using it to campaign for your favourite causes and highlight the issues, global or local, that concern you. You can find examples all over the world: young people organizing protest in Iran or Burma, animal lovers in the United States campaigning to save the wild mustangs, or mothers in Australia rousing opposition to giant phone masts overshadowing the schoolyard.

This chapter will examine the power of social networking media in promoting good causes. Charities and political organizations have already become wise to the potential of such sites – and of course our inboxes have long been bombarded with those irritating chain e-mails, usually prefaced with a note from a friend saying 'I don't normally forward these things but...', begging us to save the planet or whatever by forwarding the message to seven other people. (Personally those go straight into my spam bin, no matter how good the friend and how worthy the cause.)

Promote your cause through social networks

There are ways of using social networks online to promote more individual causes effectively – those issues dear to your heart that don't always have the back-up of a big organization to make the point. In this chapter two different case studies illustrate how two individuals with very different concerns used the internet to raise the profile of their campaign or cause.

CASE STUDY Florence Lawford versus
the planners

Florence Lawford lives in a leafy street in West London full of lovely old houses. The neighbourhood is so special that it has won Conservation Area status, which in the UK means that there are rules to be followed and permissions required before residents can change or embellish any part of the exterior of their properties or carry out any work to trees. It also means that any new developments must be carefully scrutinized to make sure they enhance and respect the existing look and character of the locale. But the area isn't just an enclave for the affluent middle-class; there is a mix of flats and houses including social housing, an old people's home and a hostel for refugees.

The people who live there are rightly proud of their neighbourhood, so it was something of a shock when the planning authorities, in the shape of the local council, appeared to be ignoring the rules with a large new development that would mean the old people's home and its surrounding mature trees and hedges would be replaced by a high-density housing development underpinned by a huge underground car park.

Using the online world to raise awareness

'The contract for the development was open to tender,' says Florence, 'and local people were invited to comment and vote for the different plans being proposed.' When the successful developer was announced and an exhibition was held to show residents what the new buildings would look like, it came as a shock.

As more and more information gradually came to light about the development, the residents began to realize that it would totally alter the character of the area. 'It means something when an area is designated a Conservation area,' says Florence. 'Not just in terms of how we think it will look aesthetically, but the kind of guidelines the developer must respect. These cover architectural style and aesthetics, environmental concerns, the types of finishes on buildings and windows, as well as skylines and particularly in this case, the building line: how far off the pavement the buildings are positioned. This was a grotesque piece of architecture that wasn't even a bespoke piece of work. It had been lifted from a development that had already been completed in East London and had then been tweaked and plopped in here.'

Another very important issue was how the development would affect the natural environment. The site was a leafy green space with many mature trees. 'They were intending to clear the site, cutting the mature trees down, eventually to be replaced with much smaller trees in submerged tubs, which would have required expensive ongoing maintenance. It would have been a terrible waste.' The plans were not yet a fait accompli – although the developer had won the tender in outline, the detailed plans still had to win final approval from the local authority's Planning Committee. The area had a newly constituted Residents Association and Florence, who felt very strongly about the proposed development, joined forces with them. At first they began campaigning by conventional means.

Collect e-mail addresses

'We started out in the neighbouring streets knocking on doors,' she says, 'gathering support and e-mail addresses as we went. Knowing that the Planning Application would go before the Council Committee, we had to get as many people as possible to write in and object, instead of ignoring what they saw as just another bit of paper coming through the door. We had to make sure that they understood what it meant for the area, and that they would respond and not just sit back and do nothing.'

So far, so conventional. However, the Residents Association felt they needed more visibility. Florence had an idea how they could bring that about.

Plan a social network

'It wasn't just our site that the Council was trying to develop in this underhanded way. I realized that there were many instances of similar things happening around the Borough. There were many other residents groups and people struggling with planning issues, but we needed to join forces and widen the campaign so that the bigger picture would be exposed and the Council forced to listen to us. We thought online social networking could allow that to happen, so I registered with Facebook and set up a page called the Hammersmith Grapevine. That way we could keep people informed about what was going on with our development and anything else that might be linked in.'

During their door-to-door campaign, they had had the foresight to collect e-mail addresses, so that gave their online campaign a good start. They wanted people to let their friends know what was going on, and spread the message virally. They designed the page to look as visually dramatic as possible, with plenty of photos, especially of the site as it was, with its mature, leafy trees.

Use pictures and photographs

'It was a way of recording which trees were under threat. It had been very difficult to find out from the Council which, if any, of the trees were protected by a Tree Preservation Order and once a development begins trees are often 'lost' because of root disturbance or heavy machine damage. Establishing that they are there in the first place is important. Then we included pictures of what the proposed development was going to look like, as well as a photographic documentary record of the different stages of fighting the development: us standing on the steps of the Town Hall with a few placards looking angry, shots of our petition being handed over. And of course there was the opportunity for anyone to post a comment, and for us to keep people informed and up to date with the campaign.'

They considered also organizing an online petition, but they felt that a physical pile of paper with hundreds of signatures on it had a greater symbolic force. Indeed, although online petitions can be very effective, people often feel inundated with online requests to sign up for this and that, and can easily ignore the call to action. The residents felt it was vital to conduct the campaign on all fronts – out in the streets and through the media as well as online.

'So we stood at the park gates and we stood at the bus stops and we stood at the street corners. We walked around all the houses in the evening when we knew people would be home, and collected signatures.' They had checked online to find the proper format to follow for a petition to be taken notice of, making sure it had a clear statement of what people are signing up to at the top of every sheet.

E-mail press campaign

At the same time they organized an e-mail campaign to press the Council under the UK Freedom of Information (FOI) Act to reveal information about traffic flow and other matters which the local authority needed to take into account before they could pass the application. They were also convinced that Tree Preservation Orders had once been in place on the mature trees on the site, and again persuaded conservationists to pester the council with FOI requests to discover if the Orders were still in existence.

'We eventually had to go to the Ombudsman because the Council failed to respond within the legal deadline. When we did eventually get a reply, we were told that there were so many archived documents relating to Tree Preservation Orders that the Council had deemed it would be too expensive and time-consuming to task someone with collecting all the information.'

The campaigners felt the Council was trying all sorts of sneaky tactics to push the development through fast. Although normally it takes months for a detailed planning application to get to committee stage, suddenly this application was added to the agenda for consideration at the very next meeting. An extraordinary move, taken even before the statutory consultation period had run out, and giving campaigners only a matter of weeks to assemble their case.

Call to action online

'That was an immediate call to arms. We used online communication to get everybody there at the meeting – although it can't just be online, it has to be personal as well – door knocking and street canvassing, posters and press.'

This potent combination of face-to-face contact, online social networking and traditional media can be very effective. All three can be woven together inseparably, so that in this campaign, even the posters were distributed online. 'I had a good friend who knocked up a poster for me, and established a website called **Listen2010.wordpress.com**. We linked that in with our Facebook page on the Hammersmith Grapevine, and gave people links to printable posters that they could put in their windows.'

Punching above your weight

The Listen2010 website was a particularly clever idea, as it was designed to relate to far more than just the residents' local campaign. 'It appealed to people across the whole of the UK who were fighting their own little battles, feeling that they weren't being listened to by the people in charge who were going to push unwanted ideas through come hell or high water.'

By associating themselves with a bigger movement – a nationwide swell of opinion against local authorities riding roughshod over their taxpayers – Florence and her fellows were able to punch well above their weight. 'In the end, I believe it really unsettled the Council because it made a relatively small piece of local activity appear much grander than it was,' she says. The timing of their campaign was also useful, coming as it did in the run-up to local and national elections. To the humiliation of the Conservative-led local council, the Conservative parliamentary candidate lost by a small margin, against the swing in the rest of the UK, a result that Florence is convinced was in part due to the strength of feeling stirred up by local campaigners.

The campaign has ended in victory for the residents. Although the Planning Committee approved the developer's application, they have now done a U-turn and decided to develop the site in a completely different way, claiming that post-election cuts have forced a rethink. Florence, however, believes that it was the action taken by the residents that finally convinced the Council to look again at the plans. 'They have realized that the way they conducted that whole consultation process was badly handled. It didn't serve their purpose, it just created an enormous conflict and bad feeling that was completely unnecessary. Had they done it in a different way and listened in the first place, they would have been much better off.'

Nuts and bolts of raising the profile of *your* campaign

There are a number of useful tips that arise from the way Florence and her fellow residents organized their campaign:

- Gather as many e-mail addresses as you can so that you have a 'core' constituency to contact once the campaign is up and running online.

- Use Facebook to network with people about the campaign. You will need one person from the campaign to take responsibility for this as Facebook only takes registrations from individuals, and requires them to supply a real address and other contact details. Then give your page visual impact by filling it with photographs and other material that illustrates what your campaign is about. You could also create a short video, upload it to YouTube, and create a link to it from your Facebook page.

- Give people a means of commenting on your cause, and don't forget to keep the page up to date as the campaign develops. As with all online activity, you have to devote time and energy to maintaining your online connections, and that's particularly important when you are trying to drum up support for a campaign or cause.

- Link to a website that will give people the opportunity to download and print well-designed posters they can display in their windows.

- If you are organizing a local campaign and you want to punch above your weight, affiliate to a website whose aims are similar but whose scope is nationwide, or even global. It is this power of linkage that makes the internet such a potent tool for campaigners. Look for other campaigns and causes that are sympathetic and willing to support you – and in turn, promote and support them via your own website or Facebook page.

- Use e-mail campaigns to swell support, especially if you need to raise numbers in a hurry for a public meeting.

- Organize e-mail campaigns to bombard the authorities with Freedom of Information requests to support your case. Although this did not succeed in eliciting the information Florence and her fellow residents wanted, it did show the Council how many people were concerned about the development, and gave the campaigners an opportunity for further press publicity when they took the Council to the Ombudsman for not responding when they should have.

- The most effective campaigns combine online networking with face-to-face contact. There is a place for both, and they can enrich and enhance each other. Don't forget you need a way of gathering those e-mail addresses in the first place!

Petitions online

Florence's group decided against organizing an online petition, as they felt that a physical petition was more convincing and gave them more opportunity to be visible locally, by being out and about on the street in their neighbourhood and creating a media photo opportunity when they handed in the petition to the local authority. Nevertheless, online petitions are a growing way of showing support for a particular cause. They can be particularly effective if your campaign has more than local resonance and you want to find out how many people support your views all over the country or all over the world.

If you are planning your petition online you have a variety of options to choose from. Here's how to organize one:

- The simplest way of creating an online petition is by posting your petition online so that the petition form can be printed off by your supporters and then used to collect signatures. Make sure you follow the rules. The top of the page needs to explain what the signature is for, and there should be space for the signature and their full name and address.

- Slightly more sophisticated is an e-mail chain letter. You write a campaigning e-mail and send it to someone you know encouraging them to send it on to their friends and colleagues. Slowly you build up support for your cause as the e-mail is passed from person to person. If you need to count the number of contacts it has reached you can ask those receiving the e-mail to click in to a particular website address.

- A further step would be to create a petition for visitors to your website to complete online. The standards of an e-petition are exactly the same as a paper one: you need a full name and address including the e-mail address. You will need to ask permission to use the e-mail address to contact those who have signed the petition, and you must not pass the information to other people without permission to do so – and of course the petition will not show this information online.

- There is an e-petition application on Facebook that can be added to your Facebook site where you can create petitions on issues you feel passionate about.

- There are also e-petition websites such as **Change.org**, **thePetitionSite.com**, iPetitions, GoPetitions, PetitionSpot and others. Petition hosts are external locations for the creation of a wide variety of petitions that are free and have easy-to-use systems specifically to help campaigners – they both host the petition and will help advertise the idea.

However, it is not all plain sailing – there can be problems with online petitions. The anonymous nature of the online world means that some petition signature lines use false names or unacceptable language. You don't want Mickey Mouse or Michael Jackson on your petition list. Check that your petition site has a system to remove these as soon as they are discovered. It should also have a system that removes duplicate signatures and sends each person who signs the petition a confirming e-mail.

Delivering the petition

You will want your petition to have maximum impact and, like Florence, you will probably want to have some publicity when you hand it to the people you are planning to influence. Some government agencies and officials, such as The Scottish Parliament with the e-Petitioner system and the Queensland Parliament in Australia, have adopted electronic petitioning systems as a way of displaying a commitment to their constituents and to provide greater accessibility to government operations. But don't neglect telling the traditional media what you are doing. Local issues especially can arouse plenty of interest in local newspapers, television or radio.

The human touch

Somebody once made the point that the personal is the political. Indeed this is why social networking sites like Facebook can be so very effective in drumming up support for a campaign. These sites allow you to appeal in a very personal way to others. They are in many ways less intrusive than an e-mail campaign: a page on Facebook, or a personal website, *invites people in* by asking them to follow a link, and people often respond better to that kind of approach rather than an aggressive, in-your-face hard sell. So the more personal you can make the appeal of your campaign, the more likely it is to win support.

The final case study in this book is a moving example of exactly that: an online campaign that achieved an astonishing global reach virtually by accident. No one imagined that it would be so successful in raising money, or in creating links between people all over the world. But it is, in many ways, the epitome of how online social networking changes lives.

CASE STUDY Mark Phillips sets up the
Debbie Fund

In 2006, Mark Phillips's 44-year-old wife Debbie was diagnosed with cervical cancer. Although she had had regular smear tests, by the time the cancer was spotted it was already well advanced and had spread to her ovaries and her lymph system. Debbie was taken into hospital for surgery, then had to undergo several weeks of intense chemo- and radiotherapy treatment.

Debbie was a remarkable woman. She and Mark had met at university in the early 1980s, where both had been studying law – Debbie went on to graduate brilliantly top of her year with a first class degree. She practised as a solicitor for six years, but when her first child, Katy, was born in 1990 she decided to give up work and become a full-time mother, throwing herself into school and community activities with the same zest and flair she had brought to her career. At the time she was diagnosed, her youngest child, Jack, was only 10 and his older sisters, Katy and Sarah, 15 and 12 respectively.

Start with e-mail

Mark's involvement with the online world to spread the news about his wife's illness began in a small way. Just after her first operation, every evening the phone would ring and ring with calls from friends, family and well-wishers anxious to know how she was. Mark found it physically and emotionally exhausting. 'Debbie was very popular, and having 60 phone calls a night was just not going to be manageable. So I set up an e-mail circulation list of all close friends and family, and said to everyone: "Please don't telephone, for obvious logistical reasons. I will keep you all posted".'

As time went by, the round-robin e-mail bulletins became more elaborate and detailed. 'It actually became a two-way thing,' says Mark, 'because everybody started sending me e-mails back about their emotional responses to what was going on. So effectively it began to develop a life of its own, and that e-mail list has eventually become the cornerstone of the Debbie Fund list, with over 700 names on it.'

At first the family had had hopes that Debbie would be given the all-clear once the first, intensive burst of treatment was over. But by 2008 it was clear the cancer was back and had spread to Debbie's brain. She fell into a coma, and when she finally emerged after weeks of hospitalization, the tumour and a brain haemorrhage had left her blind. Still she battled on, with extraordinary courage, refusing to give in. But 14 months later, after two further courses of chemotherapy, Debbie died, in February 2010.

For all Debbie's children, watching their mother fade away over the long months of her final illness was devastatingly hard. Sarah, now 16, found herself playing over and over again one song on her favourite album by Paolo Nutini, 'Autumn'. 'In the weeks running up to her death, it was one of few comforts to me,' she says.

On the evening of Wednesday 10 February, as her mother lay dying, Sarah picked up her mobile phone and, unaccompanied and note-perfect, sang 'Autumn' into it. 'It was a momentary escape, which even now is difficult to explain. It has a line in the lyric which has always struck me with especial force: "You still live on in my father's eyes".' Just over four hours later, in the early hours of Thursday 11th, Debbie died.

The family had known for a long time that Debbie's illness was terminal, so Mark had been planning the funeral for months. He had commissioned a professional film editor to compile a video tribute to Debbie, and by the Saturday after Debbie's death, all the arrangements had been made. 'On the Saturday evening, Sarah said to me, "Daddy, I want to sing at Mummy's funeral. But I don't think that I would be able to do it live, so I want to record something".' Mark was completely flummoxed. 'My immediate reaction was how on earth could I arrange this in time? I'd no idea what to do.'

Using professional help

However, chance lent a hand. The following day, at his son's football match, Mark and Sarah got talking on the touchline with the father of one of Jack's team-mates, Charlie Mole, who composes film music and has many connections in the recording business. He offered to help, and asked Sarah to send him the mobile phone recording of 'Autumn'. When he heard it, he was bowled over by the beauty of her voice and the extraordinary quality of the recording.

'We had an e-mail from Charlie that said: "We don't need to re-record this, what Sarah has done is amazing",' Mark recalls. 'We played it at the funeral when we carried Debbie into the church, and we also dubbed it onto the end of the tribute film, over family holiday video footage.' Charlie

Mole had added a backing accompaniment, and Sarah's voice, perfectly pitched yet full of the raw emotion she had felt the night her mother died, moved many of the mourners to tears. Afterwards, a number of people told Mark how much they had loved her performance of the song and asked for a copy. 'So that left me with the problem of how to get a copy out to everyone who wanted it.'

Mark asked the film editor who had cut Debbie's tribute whether he would be able to make a copy of the last three minutes of the film, with Sarah's voice singing 'Autumn' over it. He and Sarah decided to upload it to YouTube and send the link to everyone on the e-mail list.

Sharing your emotional experience

'Sarah had never uploaded anything. She didn't have a YouTube account, and the first two or three tries just didn't work at all. But eventually she cracked it, and put the video up. At the funeral, we'd asked people to donate money to University College London's Cancer Institute, to help fund research into cervical cancer. I suggested to Sarah that we should put a link from the YouTube video to the UCL website, and if people wanted to give something, then they could. So that was really what triggered the whole of the online Autumn Campaign.'

Mark had assumed that they were simply giving family and friends a way of hearing his daughter's song again. 'After the first night, Sarah had about 400 hits, and we thought, that's about right. There were roughly 400 people at the funeral, so everyone is now able to get hold of it. And then a couple of days later, the numbers had gone to a couple of thousand. There were comments, too, lovely comments from people that we didn't know. Then we had a phone call from the Chief Correspondent of The Sunday Telegraph, who told me they'd seen the video and they wanted to do a piece on it.'

Publicity

Mark's immediate reaction was to shy away from media publicity. But the senior *Telegraph* journalist convinced him otherwise. 'He said, "I don't think you really understand. If we put this in the national press, you are going to raise tens of thousands that you would not otherwise raise".' And so it proved – only the journalist had his sums wrong. The resulting coverage raised not tens of thousands, but hundreds of thousands of pounds. After the story was featured in the newspaper, Sarah's version of 'Autumn' became an internet hit. 'We looked at the YouTube site and it was clocking up 10,000 visits an hour. Then *The Daily Mail* picked it up, and all the TV channels began featuring it on their news programmes. It was even on television in Vietnam. It got picked up globally and then it went bananas.'

Donations were rolling in to the UCL site. Somebody started a Facebook campaign to have the song released as a single. A recording industry manager came across it, and enabled it to be released and sold via iTunes. It went to number 11 in the iTunes chart and to 49 in the official UK singles chart. The YouTube video eventually notched up over 380,000 hits and, with the help of Charlie Mole, Sarah has written and recorded a follow-up single, 'Blue Chair'. Meanwhile Paolo Nutini invited Sarah to his concert at London's Albert Hall, where a collection was taken for what had by now become the Debbie Fund.

An official website

With such a phenomenal success on his hands, Mark launched an official website, **www.debbiefund.org**. With the support of many sponsors, it promotes further fundraising activity to help research at UCL into drug therapy for cervical cancer. There has been a glittering Debbie Fund Ball, and elder daughter Katy has run with others in the London Marathon for the charity. To date, hundreds of thousands of pounds have been raised through the Fund, much of which was as a direct result of Sarah's recording.

Mark freely admits, 'I'm a very driven person and I have a target.' Cervical cancer is the second most common female cancer worldwide. There are around half a million new cases diagnosed each year – and a quarter of a million deaths. The five-year survival rate is about 64 per cent. Mark and his family were shocked to realize, after Debbie had been given a terminal diagnosis, that there was no dedicated drug development research programme anywhere in the world aimed specifically at finding new treatments for cervical cancer. The UCL Cancer Institute has put together a programme to establish a research group to do just that, and the money raised by the Debbie Fund will be used to support new posts for scientists at the Institute to set the programme in motion. 'UCL have some brilliant people,' says Mark, 'and they have said to me, if you give us the money we are confident we will find a drug.'

'I hope one day,' says Sarah, 'that a lady will come up to me and tell me that she had cervical cancer, but because of a drug that came out of our research, she survived.'

It's a wonderful memorial to Debbie. But the website has done more than just raise money for a deserving cause. 'We've formed an extraordinary relationship with the people who have seen the video and left comments,' says Mark. 'One guy told us that he was in his mid-30s, and he had found out that day his wife had terminal cervical cancer. He was sitting watching our video with his nine-year-old son curled up on his lap, sobbing. Sarah always tries to respond, and a few months later he sent us another e-mail to say that his wife had died. Or there was the 13-year-old boy who told us he'd just lost his mum to cancer. Husbands, wives, so many people have been affected by Sarah's recording. I've even been to meet some of them.'

With such people in mind, the Debbie Fund website contains links to another individual charity, Jo's Cervical Cancer Trust. This provides easily accessed information and support, 24 hours a day, to women and their families affected by cervical cancer and abnormalities. Their aim is that no one should ever feel alone at any stage of their journey through the illness.

'Sarah's song "Blue Chair" starts with the line: "Alone, but together. Alone not forever",' says Mark. 'It's what it's about – the impact of these communications on the grieving process, which has come about through the whole YouTube thing. Did you see that guy in New Zealand, a cancer patient who did an amazing video for his wife for her birthday? I got in touch with him right away. You can share what you're going through with men and women all over the world, who are themselves undergoing similar experiences. It helps you but it also helps other people. People are doing it together, and supporting each other.'

Action for getting a result

- Use Facebook to network with people about the campaign.

- Facebook only takes registrations from individuals, so one person must be in charge.

- Create visual impact by using photographs and other material that illustrates what your campaign is about.

- Add a short video, upload it to YouTube, and create a link to it from your Facebook page.

- You have to devote time and energy to maintaining your online connections.

The final word
on you.com

Mark and his family's story really sums up what this book is really about. There has been a revolution in the way we communicate, and it is even changing the way in which we relate to each other and the bonds we can form with total strangers the world over. Wherever there is an internet connection you will find people using social networking online to make new relationships, support each other and enrich their lives.

My hope is that this book has given you some inkling of the ways in which you can join them. If you haven't done it before, it can seem nerve-wracking, but it's actually very easy. Sarah had never used YouTube to upload a video, and it took her a good few tries to get it right, but she persevered and refused to be daunted by the technicalities. Let her example inspire you to find your own new ways of reaching out online, and remember that it is the ability to *link everything together* that is the real brilliance of online social networking. It often strikes me as being rather like three-dimensional chess, working on different levels but able to move between them – only, thankfully, online networking is not anything like as difficult!

You.com need not be parochial or self-centred. The global reach of this new way of communicating, and the subtleties of the linkages you can create, are staggering. With the right online tools and a good heart, not only can you rebrand your own image, you could even rebuild the world.

Index